MW00883872

THE WARRIOR'S COMPASS

Bravely Navigating Life's Journey
Into the Chaos and Complexity of the Unknown

by Scott P. Seagren

Illustrations by Melissa Wood

BALBOA.PRESS
A DIVISION OF HAY HOUSE

Copyright © 2021 Scott P. Seagren.

All rights reserved. No part of this book may be used or reproduced by any means, graphic, electronic, or mechanical, including photocopying, recording, taping or by any information storage retrieval system without the written permission of the author except in the case of brief quotations embodied in critical articles and reviews.

Balboa Press books may be ordered through booksellers or by contacting:

Balboa Press
A Division of Hay House
1663 Liberty Drive
Bloomington, IN 47403
www.balboapress.com
844-682-1282

Because of the dynamic nature of the Internet, any web addresses or links contained in this book may have changed since publication and may no longer be valid. The views expressed in this work are solely those of the author and do not necessarily reflect the views of the publisher, and the publisher hereby disclaims any responsibility for them.

The author of this book does not dispense medical advice or prescribe the use of any technique as a form of treatment for physical, emotional, or medical problems without the advice of a physician, either directly or indirectly. The intent of the author is only to offer information of a general nature to help you in your quest for emotional and spiritual well-being. In the event you use any of the information in this book for yourself, which is your constitutional right, the author and the publisher assume no responsibility for your actions.

Scripture quotations marked KJV are from the Holy Bible, King James Version (Authorized Version). First published in 1611. Quoted from the KJV Classic Reference Bible, Copyright © 1983 by The Zondervan Corporation.

Scripture quotations marked NIV are taken from the Holy Bible, New International Version®. NIV®. Copyright © 1973, 1978, 1984 by International Bible Society. Used by permission of Zondervan. All rights reserved. [Biblica]

Scripture quoted by permission. Quotations designated (NET) are from The NET Bible® Copyright © 2005 by Biblical Studies Press, L.L.C. www.bible.org All rights reserved.

Print information available on the last page.

ISBN: 978-1-9822-7521-1 (sc)
ISBN: 978-1-9822-7523-5 (hc)
ISBN: 978-1-9822-7522-8 (e)

Library of Congress Control Number: 2021920253

Balboa Press rev. date: 10/21/2021

Listen to the wind, it talks.
Listen to the silence, it speaks.
Listen to your heart, it knows."

Native American Proverb

"To be a spiritual warrior, one must have a broken heart; without a broken heart and the sense of tenderness and vulnerability, your warriorship is untrustworthy."

Chögyam Trungpa

"The only thing that makes life possible is permanent, intolerable uncertainty; not knowing what comes next."

Ursula Le Guin

THE COMPASS:

EAST: The path of possibility is clear to begin anew, again. Vision of what's possible and why it's important becomes clear.

SOUTHEAST: Unconditional Love flows outward with compassion and forgiveness, first to ourself and then to all other beings.

SOUTH: We are bathed, cleansed, and prepared for ushering in this new day from our wholehearted feminine nature.

SOUTHWEST: We co-create our path with the Universe and offer a profound prayer of gratitude. What we appreciate, appreciates.

WEST: We acknowledge the teacher in each moment and the opportunity at hand. Despite our fiercest inner critic, we remain open to outcomes, act intentionally and willingly let go of assumptions and clinging to any sense of permanence.

NORTHWEST: Full permission to fail. Messiness, shadows, and darkness are naturally a part of each day.

NORTH: The sacred, prophetic arising of the warrior calls us forth with gentle urgency.

NORTHEAST: We are interconnected with all things.

FATHER SKY: We graciously embrace the responsibility to see others as we are seen.

MOTHER EARTH: We take full responsibility for being good stewards of the land, the trees, the birds, the grasses, and all earthly resources.

CENTER: And we arrive in the center and know the place both intimately and as if for the first time. We take a courageous stand for human resilience, determination, and creativity.

TABLE OF CONTENTS

PREFACE ix

ACKNOWLEDGEMENTS xiii

INTRODUCTION 1

EAST – Rising into the New Day 31

SOUTHEAST – Feeling Unconditional Love, Compassion and Gentleness 63

SOUTH – Opening the Feminine Heart 81

SOUTHWEST – Co-creating with the Universe 99

WEST – Dreaming into the Sunset 113

NORTHWEST – Permission to Fail 131

NORTH – The Warrior Emerges 149

NORTHEAST – Oneness 187

FATHER SKY – Fully Seen 201

MOTHER EARTH – Sustenance of Life 211

CENTER – The Secret Sits in the Middle 225

EPILOGUE 245

THE WARRIOR'S COMPASS STANDING MEDITATION 247

PREFACE

I believe deeply in the interconnection between the human spirit and its fundamental nature to flourish, and the ever-evolving natural world. This book was born out of that belief and is meant to serve as a guide for thought-leaders—the men and women warriors of this time – YOU – to navigate your place courageously and intentionally in the world. It is urgent and critical that you do. The world needs you. What I've come to realize is that journeying from the known to the unknown is unsettling and I've needed a compass to find the way toward my best/true self. My hope is that my journey will serve as a compass for yours.

You picked up this book because on some level, you know two things: you are a warrior, and the world needs warriors. The demand today is for an exquisite blend of masculine and feminine qualities such as wisdom, curiosity, bravery, compassion, discipline, and service to others. Something inside you is looking for its tribe, aching for peace of mind and hunting for a practice that helps make sense of an inconceivably vast and sometimes confusing universe. This book is a response to my inner warrior's relentless, life-long search for meaning—and the acceptance that there may not be any. A paradox I'm now willing to accept.

If we are to bravely navigate our precarious world, we desperately need to think out loud with each other and listen with deep curiosity. With context, we are better able to form a common vision for an inhabitable future. And, because I suspect what we can see ahead may only expose the tip of a Titanic iceberg, we need a guide to hone our resilience, our warriorship.

Twitter-sized messages and the Facebook-paced flow of information have limited my ability to focus on reading a book for much more than 20 minutes in the last several years. If that sounds like you, I ask you to challenge yourself, find a comfortable space to sit down, put your phone on airplane mode, and take a long, deep breath in … and even longer flow out. Then start absorbing these words slowly. In total, they took over 10 years to write. Of course, the book can be read in short segments, but it asks for your full presence and a willingness to descend into the depths of who you are in this world, who you are meant to be in it and, vitally, what the world needs most in these precarious, treacherous times.

The invitation to read this book goes out equally to men and women. Men need to embrace greater feminine energy, just as women in the last several decades have sourced a more masculine energy to compete in the marketplace. I think of the qualities of masculine and feminine as separate from any gender orientation. While I often use "he" to describe the warrior, I could just as easily use "she." My intent is to extend an invitation to everyone so inclined to listen, to explore a wholeness of spirit that is fully, both masculine and feminine.

A note about capitalization: You'll notice there are times when I capitalize a word like "Love" or "Great Spirit." In these cases, capitalization denotes something unique, spiritual, and divine about the concept being presented. For example, the idea of "love" expresses the quality of deep care, compassion, and kinship from a human perspective which, while beautiful and fulfilling is limited by its humanity. By contrast, the idea of "Love" denotes unconditional care, endless compassion and oneness that is more universal and expansive, or divine. One isn't better or more right than the other. They both are part of our human experience as spiritual beings.

The stories inside are deeply personal. I share them in hopes that they will inspire something deeply personal in you to arise, begin a long-awaited training, clothe yourself with compassion and insight, and step fully into your spiritual warriorship. Here may we find our right relationship with all the world.

ACKNOWLEDGEMENTS

There are many teachers who influenced the building of the model I present in this book. Some know what a profound effect they had on me, and others likely have no idea. Specifically, I thank Angeles Arriens, albeit posthumously, for her book, *The Fourfold Path.* Without it I wouldn't have learned the sacredness of the compass directions. I also acknowledge don Miguel Ruiz and his book, *The Four Agreements,* without which I wouldn't have learned the commitments needed in the four directions. Chögyam Trungpa's book, *Shambhala: The Sacred Path of the Warrior,* filled in many of the blanks for me about spiritual warriorship.

Much of the metaphysical basis for this journey was developed in my childhood, being raised as a Christian Scientist. The writings of the founder, Mary Baker Eddy and the Bible were a daily source of inspiration for many years and were foundational to my belief that each of us at our core is naturally whole, good, and well-designed. In these teachings, I also became familiar with the idea that what we hold in thought generally manifests itself outwardly at some point in our experience.

In 2007, I signed up for a Leadership Development program taught by very insightful people at the Co-Active Training Institute. My leaders in the course, brothers Pat Carrington-House and Henry Kimsey-House, offered a way to see how our world can be one of our choosing if only we would take responsibility for the impact we have on it—the journey of the conscious leader. Their guidance and challenge to take full responsibility for my impact on the world led me to believe I have a voice that needs to be spoken out loud. Years later, reading Richard Rohr's teachings on Order-Disorder-Reorder sustained me as my belief systems transformed.

In Pema Chödron and the Shambhala tradition of warriorship I found comfort and inspiration. Their writings felt like old friends with whom I was being reacquainted and I cuddled especially close to them in my darkest moments. They described the warrior who was at once courageous and tender—masculine qualities made whole by their counterbalancing feminine qualities; the warrior who stands at the confluence of heaven and earth, being both spiritual and human; and the warrior who is both alone and deeply interconnected with everything.

In 2015-16, I joined Meg Wheatley's "Warrior's for the Human Spirit" training just outside Zion National Park in Utah. Along with amazing teachers Jerry Granelli, Barbara Bash, Ulrike Ebert and Alan Sloan, our cohort gathered to discover how to build resilient warriorship through meditation, deep conversations, calligraphic brush painting, and Qigong training. Most profound in this training was taking this vow spoken by Chögyam Trungpa: "I cannot change the way the world is, but by opening to the world as it is, I may discover that gentleness, decency and bravery are available not only to me but to all human beings." My warriorship would not be where it is today without this deep, humbling, and challenging training.

We are all the hero of our own mythical journey. Joseph Campbell and Carl Jung wrote extensively on the patterns of narrative along this journey. My "hero's journey" was widely informed and validated by these authors. Navigating my adventure was important for my sanity and desire to make meaning of my experiences. But the archetype of the hero offers a bigger purpose to going out and slaying one's dragons—doing so *on behalf of the tribe.* That element of service is what compels me to share my learning with you.

Along the way, I found honing my warriorship was not merely a self-reflective, intellectual practice. Physically embodying the journey was the only way to have it become fully integrated into my being. Perhaps because I was always an athlete, I needed to build muscle memory to retain my learning. I started practicing yoga, Tai Chi and Qigong—ancient practices formed to build resilience, groundedness, and a melding of inner and outer. I deeply appreciate all the teachers of these practices along the way—some in person, some through on-line courses, and some who unknowingly taught me just through my observation of their practice.

Most of my heroes and role models, including Gandhi, the Dalai Lama, William Wallace, Abraham Lincoln, Black Elk, Martin Luther King, Jr., Jesus, and Siddhartha, embraced the strengths of both masculine and feminine qualities. Such polarities are central to the symmetry of the model I share here. Compassion and courage, water and fire, and acceptance and claiming are integral to its power. Willingness to accept polarities and paradox is a key trait of the leaders who can build a sustainable future.

As my own acceptance of paradox grew, I started seeing it all around me. My love of business led me to Dee Hock, founder, and CEO of what was to become Visa International, who coined the idea of a "Chaordic Organization" at the Santa Fe Institute in 1993.[1] Essentially, he described systems that are at once both chaotic and ordered. That paradox spoke to me as key to the kind of leadership needed for the world we are creating from today forward.

Many people have helped me along the way to bringing this book from journal entries and early writings to book form. I appreciate the challenge to be a better writer from my college professors Colin Campbell at Principia College and Elizabeth Dipple at Northwestern University as well as current-day editors Joann Dobbie and Sherry Law. My most thoughtful, supportive editor who always champions and challenges me to speak from my true voice, is my wife Trinnie Houghton. Illustrations in this book are from long-time friend Melissa Wood.

Finally, and probably most importantly, I want to acknowledge the teachers I find every day in my clients. It is an incredible,

---

[1] For details on how he came to this idea, see "The Art of Chaordic Leadership" by Dee Hock in Leader to Leader, No. 15 Winter 2000, available on the Drucker Foundation website www.drucker.org.

sacred privilege to sit with leaders to listen, guide and learn from them as a leadership coach. They likely will never know just how much I learn about humility, true entrepreneurship, confidence, being with and recognizing the stories we tell ourselves, and what it means to integrate family life, work life and everything in-between.

Scott Seagren, July 2021

INTRODUCTION

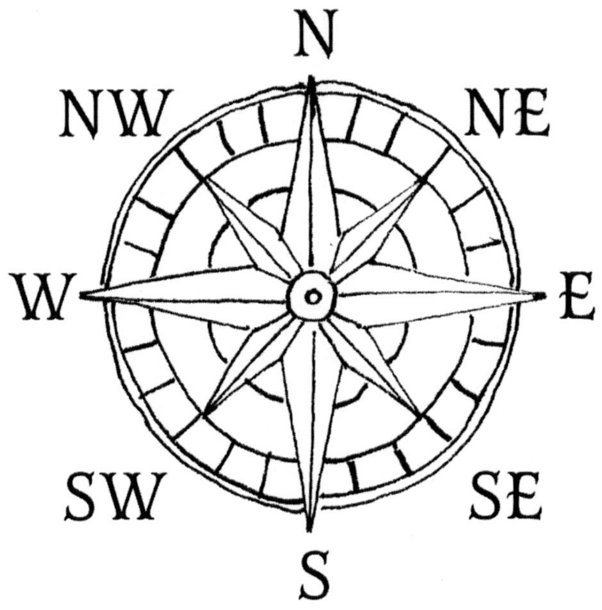

Quotes for the Introduction:

"For us, warriors are not what you think of as warriors. The warrior is not someone who fights ..." – Sitting Bull

"The ultimate measure of a man is not where he stands in moments of comfort and convenience, but where he stands at times of challenge and controversy." – Martin Luther King, Jr.

A Warrior's Work

Thought leaders are modern day warriors, but not the kind of warrior you might think. They look forward for the sake of the whole, while willingly stand alone on a precipice of uncertainty. They take a stand for independent thinking while taking the risk of being marginalized. They speak up and speak out when everyone one else is silently stuck in a narrowing perspective. They courageously step forward, charting a path for others despite unknown outcomes. Forward thinking is a vital role in organizations, places of worship, families, and political systems that spend too much time slaving over what worked in the past at the expense of innovating what will serve the future.

The thought leader who takes responsibility for his impact also embraces the ancient warrior's qualities of courage, strength, stamina, discipline, risk-taking, and determination. The warrior of old was a combatant fit for war and fully prepared to die in battle. Imagine what it took to become a brave warrior: the daily honing of skills through rigorous competition and practice, exercise and challenge and a willingness to leave behind conventional life and comfort for the sake of the whole. In the same way, the modern-day warrior and thought leader must also be fit for leading a world besieged by terrorism, failed policies, and environmental decay.

Vulnerability is a well-known friend for the spiritual warrior. The Cambridge Dictionary definition of vulnerable is, "*able to be easily physically, emotionally or mentally hurt, influenced or attacked."* Trained warriors know their exposure to harm or even death and willingly fight from that place. To be vulnerable is to be simultaneously, and paradoxically, exposed, and safe. Isn't that the place in which we all find ourselves today? We know we're exposed, and somewhere, deep inside, we also know we'll figure things out.

Today's warrior holds paradox as normal and acceptable. The warrior knows that getting attached to his position invites *intolerance, fear,* and *aggression.* The modern-day warrior's work is to quickly recognize when these elements creep into his perspective and recover to neutral ground where he can live alongside *tolerance, love, and humility.* The most original work of many thought leaders is born from the paradox of possibility and potential—and sadness and disappointment. Their work is both a calling and an acceptance of responsibility for the rippling impact on many, many people.

Another term that describes the kind of leader/warrior I describe here, is "spiritual warrior." These warriors challenge internal fear, judgment and suffering and stay with the consequential discomfort. Too often we run away from uneasiness or simply marginalize it so much it just comes back disguised in other forms such as health issues and feelings of being stuck, desperate, or depressed. The warrior spirit always strives for more awareness, more emotional intelligence, more compassion, and more unconditional love, while also accepting their weaknesses and shortcomings.

This spirit drives and inspires leaders to make a difference in their world, one that isn't limited by size or importance. That world can be defined by the walls of a home, a community, an organization, or all of humanity.

Staying present, open, and grounded is the most vital task of the day for those who serve others. The capacity to engage with the world in an authentic way is the work of today's thought-leaders and warriors—those willing to speak up, name what they see, and do something about it.

Today's warrior expresses many qualities as they go about their work. But two qualities stand out to me, both of which are required: courage and bravery. I remember reading a definition of bravery somewhere as the ability to confront something difficult, dangerous, or painful without fear. Courage is often described similarly as the ability to confront the pain, difficulty, and danger, but is differentiated as a quality or choice that is made *despite any fear* and is often compelled by a cause. I chose the word "Bravely" in the title of this book because while a courageous heart is most definitely needed, it is a courage that arises from an inner, fearless knowing that one is called into service. There is a certain sense of knowing that accompanies the difficult, painful work. It is that knowing that appears as fear-less and is most closely associated with the Warrior I speak of in this book.

Increasing volatility, uncertainty, complexity, and ambiguity, referred to in the last decade as a VUCA world, require a warrior's fearless, deft hand and a courageous, resilient heart. In 2020, living in an uncertain world is a gross understatement to the sea-changes and fundamental shifts we're experiencing worldwide. Using this compass as a guide, I got to know my inner warrior and began leveraging the innate qualities of bravery, courage, curiosity, discipline, and service, and navigate the increasing feeling of being utterly lost. Along the way, I found this beautiful poem as a deep comfort:

> *Stand still. The trees ahead and bushes beside you*
> *Are not lost. Wherever you are is called here,*
> *And you must treat it as a powerful stranger,*
> *Must ask permission to know it and be known.*
> *The forest breathes. Listen. It answers,*
> *I have made this place around you,*
> *If you leave it you may come back again, saying Here.*
> *No two trees are the same to Raven.*
> *No two branches are the same to Wren.*
> *If what a tree or a bush does is lost on you,*
> *You are surely lost. Stand still. The forest knows*
> *Where you are. You must let it find you.*[2]

An Urgent Need for Brave Leaders

I was compelled to write this book after 30 years of building a daily "grounding" practice while navigating my life as a commodities trader, family-raiser, spiritual healer,

[2] From the poem "LOST," by a Native American Elder on the matter of waking up and saving our lives, translated by David Wagoner. (U of Washington)—Taken from David Whyte's book "The Heart Aroused," page 261.

international adventurer, and executive coach and guide to hundreds of leaders and their teams. My life practice has matured, contracted, stagnated, imploded, and evolved many times over those years. Today, this practice follows the form of a holistic compass which grows and guides me every day. I share it as a tool to help you find a way to stay grounded and inspired as you, too, deal with the increasing complexity and chaos of a noisy world.

It seems the noise of climate disruption and political disenchantment has only just begun. I suspect things will only get noisier and more vicious storms will rage on with increasing destructiveness. I began to write this book as a way of processing how I could help in the presence of such uncertainty, chaos, and fear. What I found was an inner knowing that helped me confront the fear of not knowing what was next. Whereas for the first part of my life, I felt grounded on what I did know and what I was certain about, increasingly, I became compelled to respond to the growing desperation from a place of not knowing exactly what to do in the face of all the noise.

I used to think as I became more successful, life would become less complex. If only I had enough victories I could rest from the daily stresses of business and personal life. Then, in 2009, I was introduced to the theories of adult development. Like babies who move from crawling to walking to running, adults also experience levels of development. The adult's levels, however, are all present, all the time – we just happen to find ourselves in various *states* of development minute by minute, whether we are aware or not. Raising consciousness is about knowing where we are at the present moment, what might be needed to create a certain outcome, and recovering quickly to the most effective state for the issue at hand. Not surprisingly, each state allows the aware adult to deal with greater levels of complexity and exposes them to more opportunities for success and failure.

This was a radical departure from thinking my world would get less complex as I progressed in my abilities and experience. Navigating these states became my new pathway to staying just ahead of being overwhelmed by the distress and sadness of a tangled, often disappointing world. I needed a guidance system to help me confidently navigate the complex path from unconscious to conscious leadership – what seemed to me the antidote for blindly slaving to a past inadequately designed for a disruptive and chaotic future.

I began by paying keen attention to what current leaders were doing to navigate their ever-changing landscapes. Leadership effectiveness is often measured by a leader's ability to navigate a strategy from current reality to a future goal and set a direction for their followers. They often use some form of GPS (Global Positioning System) to set a course to profitability in their organizations, with a dashboard showing metrics and economic indicators against current revenues and budgeted forecasts. To operate effectively, a GPS unit needs two inputs: current location and a destination point. In business parlance, current account balances and accurate forecasts.

With any kind of movement, the GPS allows for corrections to the route along the way. It is interactive, unbiased, and non-judgmental. Were it only so simple and accessible to navigate leadership!

GPS provides a basis for understanding. It works from a built-in compass to get successfully from point A to point B, but it is not an effective tool if the route is complex. Likewise, business and thought leaders share the need for inner guidance as they chart unknown territory – a landscape of the mind that can only be navigated with a reliable compass, but one capable of handling complexity. Unlike GPS systems, conscious leaders don't necessarily just aim at a point in the distance and begin moving. They must learn to find their footing and compass headings on ever-changing ground. These leaders consider context (where they are) equal to, if not more important than, content (what they're doing). It's urgent that today's conscious leaders hold the current predicament as a point in time, prioritizing the method of travel over the actual destination.

I use this compass as a navigation tool since my model isn't content-oriented. If there's no magnetic interference, a compass shows the user only the context, which direction is north for example. It is not interactive and doesn't change its purpose or direction. Never have leaders needed such an inner guidance system. We all have this inner compass, but do we know how to read it and track it, and how to act as a result? The leaders who can build a sustainable future will be defined by their willingness to accept polarities and paradox. They'll embody compassion and courage, acceptance and claiming as integral to their power. They will also be guided by an inner calling.

My Journey as Silver Fox

My curiosity and learning about warriorship began in the early '70's at a summer camp in the Ozarks of Missouri where I became fascinated with and closely identified with Native American "braves." I soon found adopted roots in the Native American tribes of the Osage, Winnebago, Chippewa, Sioux, Potawatomi, Chickasaw, and Pawnee. Many generations ago, these tribes inhabited the land on which I grew up and the legends of their tribes live on in the soil in which I played as a child, dreamed, and toiled in as an adult, and will at some point return to.

As a child, I also spent time with my dad attending "Indian Guides" meetings, a program organized through local YMCA chapters that foster a positive relationship between father and child through outdoor activities. I remember vividly sitting at the kitchen table with my dad thinking about our Indian Guide names. We tried on several variations, most of which I cannot remember today. But, when we said out loud the names "Silver Fox" for me and "Grey Fox" for him, in a moment the words captured everything I hoped to be in my life and everything life hoped me to be. Silver Fox represented an adept, flexible and cunning way of moving through life. And being called "Silver Fox" at 7 years old was intriguing. It was regal but not gaudy and both precious and durable. Finding this name made me feel like I had a purpose to live into, a calling beyond the name my parents gave me.

Carving this name into a piece of wood with a wood-burning knife was a sacred moment I had never known before. And when I hung the badge around my neck it was like an honor had been bestowed on me that I could grow into for the rest of my life. Every meeting we went to over those years I looked forward to with great anticipation… "what would Silver Fox learn about his surroundings and how to act next?" I wondered. For those many years in Indian Guides and at the summer camp in the Ozarks, I felt special, chosen, and needed. Something every child should experience at a young age.

But the years went on and I grew up, mostly forgetting my ceremonial name until I signed up for a Leadership Development course in 2007. Seated in a large circle, the leaders of the course introduced themselves with their ceremonial names. Instantly, an inner memory chord chimed. I remembered in an instant that I was *Silver Fox* and for the rest of the year long program, all the glory of that name came back to me. I could see how, over the years since putting that badge around my neck, I had lived much of the name's calling. And then it was time for a new name as if a chapter in a book was ending. A new calling and an expanded purpose awaited.

Three Owls Emerges

Around my 45th birthday, Pat Carrington-House (one of the Leadership Development group co-leaders) helped me design a "Journey Shield" ceremony for me to perform by myself on my land in Nebraska to mark the significance of crossing a threshold from the first half to the second half of my life. Naming and claiming the formative components of the first half of my life allowed a new name to come to life. It was on that land in 2007 that I found my new name, *Three Owls*. The full detail of how this name came to be and its significance is shared in the Southeast chapter. This name has great significance in the *Warrior's Compass,* and it continues to teach me who I am to be in this world every day. Little did I know at the time just how life changing that moment would be as nearly everything I knew was turned upside down over the following few years.

Over my life to date, three significant events have tempered my inner warrior. In 1990, my mother passed away after a hard-fought bout with cancer that she kept mostly to herself. In early 2004, my decades long business partnership with my father unraveled. In 2010, my twenty-three-year marriage dissolved. Each of these experiences met me at different stages of my practice and formed a slice of how I saw the world. Sadness, grief, loss, and darks nights of the soul became my teachers. As I fully leaned into each lesson, it became part of the fabric of my being. I realized I was living out the pattern of the soul Richard Rohr articulates as a common pattern to life he calls "Order-Disorder-Reorder," several times through.

My view of the universe needed to be rebuilt piece by gut-wrenching piece as my belief systems unraveled and my support systems fell apart. This compass is the result of my metamorphosis. It's what sustained me and allowed me to find my place in one of the "Reorder" parts of my life, as *Three Owls*.

Birth of My Inner Warrior

I now know that the development of our inner warrior is not, and never will be, comfortable. Rather, it is often excruciating and exhausting. I learned that's what makes it a warrior's journey. My inner warrior was birthed into the world from the darkness, pain, and messiness of traumatic difficulty – all to bring my gifts to fruition.

Slowly, and perhaps unwillingly, I began to appreciate that broken heartedness and sadness are essential qualities of true warriorship. Craving solid ground while my well-known and trusted external support systems crumbled, I discovered an interior landscape of "primordial confidence," as described by Chögyam Trungpa in *Shambhala: The Sacred Path of the Warrior*:

> *From the great cosmic mirror*
> *Without beginning and without end,*
> *Human society became manifest.*
> *At that time liberation and confusion arose.*
> *When fear and doubt occurred*
> *Towards the confidence which is primordially free,*
> *Countless multitudes of cowards arose.*

When the confidence which is primordially free
Was followed and delighted in,
Countless multitudes of warriors arose.
Those countless multitudes of cowards
Hid themselves in caves and jungles...
Of those who were dedicated to the primordial confidence,
The many hosts of warriors,
Some went to highland mountains
And erected beautiful castles of crystal.
Some went to the lands of beautiful lakes and islands
And erected lovely palaces...
They were always without quarrel,
Ever loving and generous.

Reading this poem again after the tumultuous events in 2020, it seems even more apropos to lean into the warriors who must naturally arise. What really stood out to me was the phrase, "primordial confidence." Primordial is something that has existed since the beginning of time. So, imagine a confidence that has always been intact. One that is "ever loving and generous." That's the kind of warrior needed today. No egoistic building up of personal self-confidence but a foundational knowing that deep interconnection with everything is paramount to the identity of these warriors. Feeling this warriorship rising within me, inspired me to be even more of service and trusted as a guide to leaders, in fact, a leader of leaders.

The warriors I speak of in this book, the modern-day warriors, are compassionate and gentle but not soft and weak. Like the practice of Tai Chi, I was building a soft exterior around a solid core like a needle wrapped in cotton.

This image of warriorship in action resonates deeply in my body. A warrior's outward gentleness is solidly grounded and comes from the acceptance of, but not the giving in to, both fear and doubt. In the Shambhala tradition, this is known as *Basic Goodness* symbolized by the *Great Eastern Sun:* true human dignity that rises new and fresh every morning and represents human awakening and the rise of human warriorship. As you read on, let your inner warrior rise. Let your basic goodness guide you gently, fiercely and with certainty. What follows is a description and illustration of the model itself.

The Warrior's Compass Model

This model tracks compass headings, a form of measurement that moves clockwise, starting from the East. Compass headings were described in the Native American tradition of the medicine wheel, sometimes called a sacred hoop, which brings a person into balance and serves as a reminder to walk in sacred balance. There are many medicine wheels in existence, each with its own balance of medicine or power. No wheel is more correct than another. What's important is that your wheel works for you. I offer this model as a medicine wheel that has worked for me. What's similar is the invitation is to find balance or integration between all parts of the wheel. When we are balanced, we naturally get much closer to others, part of being in "right" relationship. This sacred relationship is known by a sense of congruency, transparency, and easily naming what's true for each person without reprisal. Being in right relationship is mutually supportive and is vital to a warrior's survival.

The necessary components of this wheel or compass are specified by the:

- Four cardinal directions: East, South, West and North
- Three altitudinal directions: Up, Down and Center
- Three "life reference point" directions noted as "Owls" (denoted by Southeast, Northwest, and Northeast)

Like any tool, the compass is most effective when used regularly and within the context of one's whole experience, incorporating both the needs of the day and the current chapter of life in which we find ourselves. It can also be used as a meditation with various, important focus points on which to place your attention. Every time you use this tool you claim your warriorship and are fully *in* the practice, regardless of which point is your focus in the moment. The illustration below shows the basics of this compass.

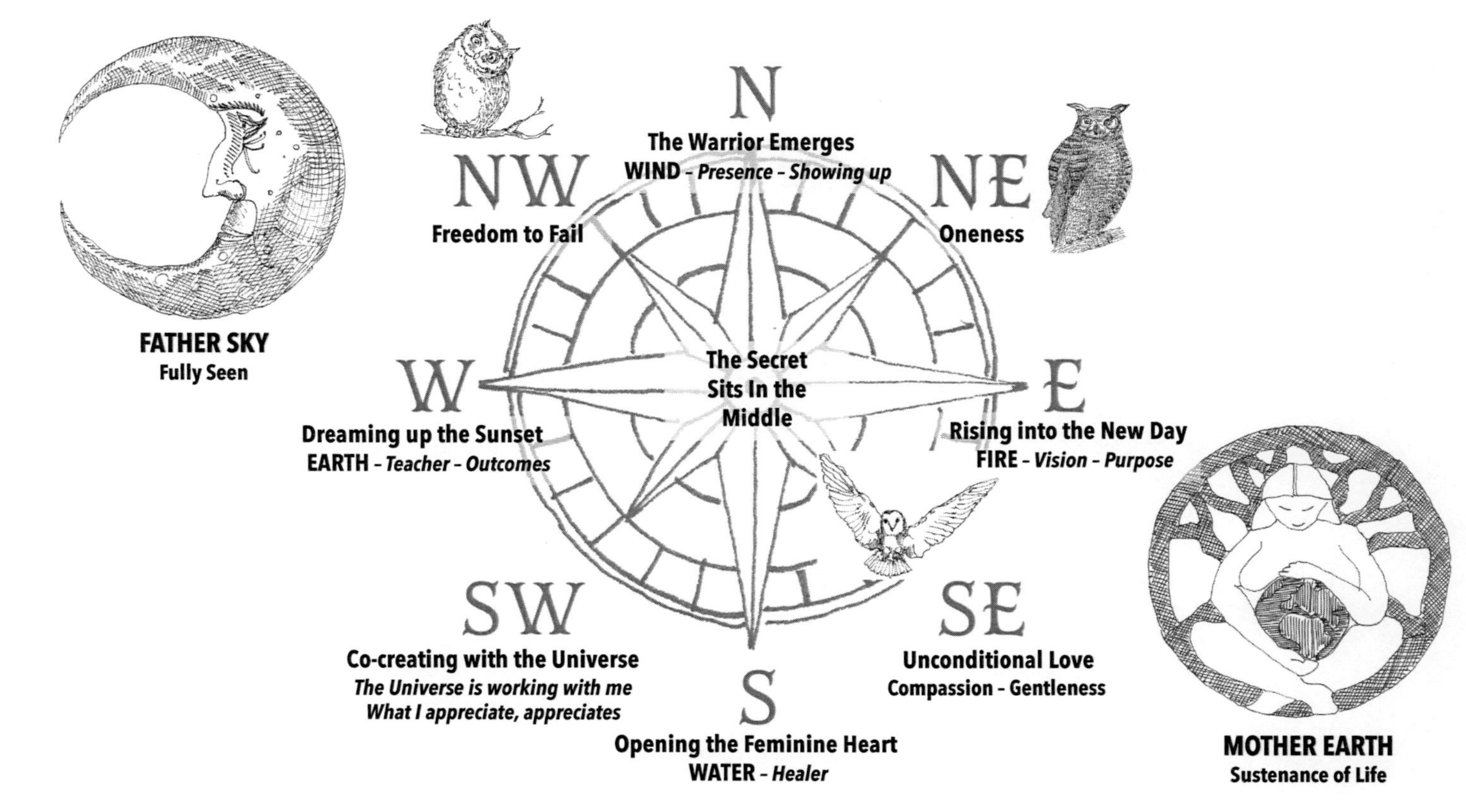

N
The Warrior Emerges
WIND – Presence – Showing up
NW
Freedom to Fail
NE
Oneness
FATHER SKY
Fully Seen
W
Dreaming up the Sunset
EARTH – Teacher – Outcomes
The Secret
Sits In the
Middle
E
Rising into the New Day
FIRE – Vision – Purpose
SW
Co-creating with the Universe
The Universe is working with me
What I appreciate, appreciates
SE
Unconditional Love
Compassion – Gentleness
S
Opening the Feminine Heart
WATER – Healer
MOTHER EARTH
Sustenance of Life

Sacred circles, according to native wisdom, are always entered from the East when in the context of our human life. This is where the sun begins its day (from the earth's perspective). As you look at the illustration, let your eyes fall on the right side first and continue around clockwise. This book is divided into chapters that correspond with the different directions of a compass, beginning with the East, the direction of renewal, birth, rebirth, and the capacity to believe in the unseen, and following around clockwise.

Moving Through the Compass

Below are descriptions of my reflection in each direction. I typically move through it as a morning meditation. While I always start in the East, I often move through the model quickly and let one of the directions "call" me for deeper focus. Sometimes this takes 3 minutes, other times it takes 30 minutes. There are weeks I practice with the compass every day, and weeks that go by without using it all the way around. On those days, I seem to know which direction will challenge me the most and linger there. Nearly every day, I, at the very least, acknowledge the sun rise in the East and take a moment to honor the new day. I find it best practiced outdoors in a natural setting. I find a quiet space where the sun is visible, even if only through a window, and locate East (using an actual compass when necessary to ensure accuracy). I get centered with both feet connected to the ground and, standing firmly, face East and begin by physically bowing into the space, honoring the sacredness of the sunrise, and connecting visually and energetically to it, and giving thanks for its presence.

To begin with, just read through each direction slowly. When finished with that direction, shift your position to the next one (physically facing that compass direction), typically about a shoulder width rotation to the right and read the next one. You'll get the essence of each direction so that eventually you can add your own points of inspiration to each direction. At one point early on, using my physical compass, I put up a picture or notation of each direction on the walls in my basement, so I knew where to focus.

The Compass Meditation:

Facing East – Rising into the New Day:

Feet shoulder-width apart, feeling them solidly on the ground. Roots from the bottom of my feet reach deep into the center of the earth. Hands low and relaxed. Chest open, shoulders back, face upward toward the early light.

Soaking in the morning sunshine, I acknowledge Spirit's warmth within, feeling the first rays of bathing light on my skin. A gentle flame is lit under my feet from the soft morning rays and quickly builds into a cleansing fire throughout my body. The fire kills off all the brushy top growth of weeds from the day before but does not consume me. I accept Great Spirit's smile on this day. Burning even more deeply into the core of my being, the sun's white-hot flames baptize every atom of me with light, from my toes to the top of my head.

On this new day, I begin again with a blank canvas on which anything is possible to be imagined. Basic Goodness is my core virtue. I was born at this moment in history to be here on this day. I re-member my life-purpose, letting it renew my calling into the day ahead.

Turning to the Southeast – The First Owl Flies in with Unconditional Love, Compassion and Gentleness:

Standing with arms outstretched, palms facing the sky, and eyes gently closed; feeling a warm, orange-hued liquid filling up the body from the toes upward, pouring out the top of the head, then back down through the fingers, and the toes, overflowing into the whole room, the house, the neighborhood, the community, down every street and into every river, expanding to the whole country, across oceans, around the world and with increasing pace, into all space ... the stars, the universe and beyond.

I am here to be a vessel of radiance – to give unselfishly and to love unconditionally. This starts with all that is good and flows through all of me: the beautiful, the shameful, the forgiven, the slightly awkward, the delightfully brilliant, and the ugly. All parts of me are included. Waves of unconditional love ripple outward, first to loved ones and family; then out to close friends; then colleagues, neighbors, and finally strangers around the world, touching every heart. I pause on each person, feeling loving kindness and compassion.

May you all be healthy. May you all find gentleness in your suffering. May you all be resilient and comforted. May you all be happy.

Facing South – Opening the Feminine Heart:

Feel the moisture all the way from the tropics wafting northward. Conspiring with the skies overhead to bring a warm rain that falls gently on my head, washes down my shoulders and arms, legs, and feet, dripping off my fingertips and out my toes, taking with it any residue of ash from the flames of the East. Drenched in these warm waters I am bathed by a source outside myself. The warmth creates a kind of Teflon mantle whereby anything that would attempt to attach itself to me (self-doubt, criticism, blame, low self-esteem, etc.) doesn't stick - it simply washes away.

Cleansed, I hear a sweet, gentle voice, saying: May all my words be spoken from love, encouragement, and empathy, mending what needs mending and giving balm to a fearful and lonely world. I feel empathy for all of life, natural and human.

I give myself to this day wholeheartedly – no reserve for fear, scarcity, or uncertainty. As a healer, I love and heal myself first. Baptized clean and free to give birth to a new day with clarity, inspiration and fresh energy, the waters flowing away from my feet grow into rivers and lakes and reservoirs of healing.

Moving toward the Southwest – Co-creating with the Universe:

I am an integral part of something much bigger than "me."

The entire Universe is working with me – creating my path just as I am creating it.

I know that what I appreciate today will appreciate.

No matter the difficulty, I carry beauty, gratitude, and confidence in my heart.

Surrender into the flow of Life.

Turning West – Dreaming up the Sunset:

Imagine the arc the sun will travel today, high overhead. Feel the rays of light blazing a trail of warmth from the bottom of the spine, up along each vertebra and up over the top of the head, lifting me up to be an inch taller. I stand on solid ground, claiming all that will be and how I want to feel at day's end.

What might the day teach me?

What do I have to teach others?

Notice – be keenly aware of the assumptions that try to take root here. I am open to all outcomes and notice when I'm overly attached to them.

I step into my brilliance. Fully embracing my potential, I know what is needed for today.

Picking up a handful of earth, as if at the end of the day, I blow it all away with a simple breath. Everything I plan for, strategize about, and envision is held so lightly that I can still be open and allow everything to unfold naturally. Like a beautifully created Mandala that is created for this moment and then released, I feel present, light, without baggage and free.

Gazing Curiously to the Northwest – The Second Owl Appears with the message of Full Permission to Fail:

I give myself full permission to suck, to mess up and make mistakes today, and all the previous days I've walked this earth.

I accept all parts of myself as necessary to be whole – light, dark, messy, brilliant and say a playful "ta daaa" when I fall into the inevitable muddy puddles. I thank them.

I embrace creativity, playfulness, and resilience today. I love you. I'm sorry. Please forgive me. Thank you.

Facing North – The Warrior fully Emerges:

The full extent of the brave, courageous and deeply compassionate masculine arises in me with a whoosh of frozen air.

Today's accomplishments are infused with resilience, honor, and dignity.

My back is strong and straight. I feel the wind pushing and pulling me about, but like Willow wedded to Oak, I am grounded by my deep roots and can sway with the wind effortlessly.

I choose to show up fully present and give my best to every endeavor. I also choose to let my belly be soft, open, and vulnerable. Courage meets compassion in a graceful balance.

I am life itself.

Turning to the Northeast – The Third Owl Appears Proclaiming Oneness:

Deeply grounded now, balanced in the paradox of polarities, dignified and open.

I know that everything – large, small, known and unknown are interconnected.

I am at one with everyone that comes into consciousness, every blade of grass, every bird's song, every grain of sand.

I am you.

You are me.

There is no separation.

We are one.

Looking UP to Father Sky – Fully Seen:

Seeing all—being seen fully and transparently by the Great Spirit of the Heavens.

The whole system is known, honored and purposeful.

Help me to see as I am seen, love as I am loved and surrender into Your arms.

Looking DOWN to Honor Mother Earth – Sustenance of Life:

Holding hands outward in a welcoming gesture. Thank you, Mother Earth, for providing the very breath of life for every bug, tree, flower, seed, bird, animal, plant, and being.

We are all blessed by your generosity, guidance, and abundance.

Center – The Secret Sits in the Middle:

Left hand over right fist, two inches below the navel – this is my center.

I notice where I stand is at the confluence—the co-incidence of heaven and earth. This is the place where humanity exists, connected above and below, supported, and seen, never alone, never disconnected.

And so, I bow to the Center where the perfect point of alignment exists.

Gathering in all the energy from the Earth below...
Gathering in all the energy from the Sky above...

I bring it up through my body while breathing in – and pushing my breath out as I raise my hands to the sky.

Then bringing all the energy from the Sky above while deeply breathing in, pulling it down through my body – and pushing my breath out loudly, giving it back to the Earth.

Rubbing both fists on my lower back (kidney area) 3 times and with a loud "Haaa," releasing all energy into the Earth.

I take in nothing extra. I am complete and have everything I need today.

I rest in the Center of the compass, fully grounded, fully prepared, fully accepting of what is.

As I bow out, I offer gratitude for receiving the blessings of awakening. In seeing every part of myself and others, we are one. Thank you.

Working through the compass points like this is often referred to in Native American terms, as *working with a medicine wheel*. I like to think of this wheel as a "*how to be with my day*" tool. Bringing a topic into the wheel often generates insight that may come in the form of a question, a vision, or a dream. Often there is an attendant and unique "spirit" animal serving as a guide at each point. Animals play an important role for the warrior. At times, the animal may act only as a metaphor, enlisting certain qualities that help with a perspective. Other times, certain animal species cross paths with unusual frequency and at opportune moments. The Owl is the totem guide on this compass and is the messenger for three directions, Southeast, Northwest, and Northeast.

Animal messengers often encourage deeper insight. In the native tradition, everything in nature—all the animals, trees, rocks, grasses, color, smell of the earth, etc.—is a messenger from the spirit world. When a certain animal or object appears more than others, it may become a talisman or totem to the person who takes notice. Pay attention to the animals that cross your daily path, especially the ones that are repetitive. Meditation on the meaning of the message from the spirit animal is another way of finding insight to the topic at hand. Some find animals to be divine messengers from God. Others simply see them as reminders to consider something deeper. Whatever they mean to you, don't get too caught up in the terminology or the emphasis on mysticism or meaning. Focus on where the thoughts take you and the realizations coming from those places.

Choose a Conscious Journey

The journey of a warrior is inevitably arduous. The warrior's only choice is whether to make the journey consciously or unconsciously. Nobody gets to make that choice for you. You choose your path in a million small decisions every day. Keep your inner compass handy to help point you toward conscious choice.

My intention in sharing this tool is to impassion your warrior practice beyond mere survival. We live in a chaotic, complex, and deteriorating world. In this place, leaders must become known as much for their listening as they are for their thought-provoking and insightful words. They must learn to love beyond family, friends, and people who think like them. Abundance and understanding must outweigh scarcity and skepticism. The most respected leaders must dare to embrace all their inner parts with candor, vulnerability, and compassion. This tool can be used to step into one's truest self and highest potential. It can also be used to shine a light on the area most in need of attention.

Warriors begin positing their perspectives and arguments at the intersection of order and chaos. They set the agenda for what our world will be like in the coming decades so it is vital to accept that while things may not be understood at this intersection, there is a powerful way to hold the uncertainty. And perhaps that is the point. To understand anything in the future takes courage to be wrong, willingness to accept the high risk of failure, and humility to keep discovering, nonetheless. Therein is the practice of thought-leadership and today's warrior.

The ideas in this book are not new. Many sage travelers have spoken various parts of them before me. And yet, for me the words and ideas are profound. They guide me beyond the more formal spiritual teachings and traditions of my elders. I am still learning to hold them all lightly by claiming a humble, "*how fascinating*" when something doesn't fit quite in the right place. The compass and my inner warrior are still my most powerful teachers of how to stay awake, and they are still a work in progress.

What are you willing to stay awake for while others are sleeping? What are you so passionate about that nothing will keep you from it? *These* are the decisions thought leaders make every day. We are all on the journey of our lives. Will you take that journey consciously or unconsciously? This is a moment-by-moment decision. I invite you to enter the sacred hoop amid your darkness, complexity, pain, chaos, and despair… and when that seductive urge to go back to sleep wrenches your equilibrium, welcome it.

This urge is a friend, an angel in disguise, a signpost reminding you that you are indeed still alive and have a unique, compelling reason to be here. Life wants something from you. Stay with the darkness as much as the light. The faint rays of a new day will begin, and the splendor of another sunrise will reassure you that you've chosen well. Now take a moment to consider why this book has come to you at this time and in this place, set a powerful intention for reading it, and let's be on with it.

EAST

Rising into the New Day

ELEMENT: *Fire*

Fire is thought to be the first element born when the universe was created. It symbolizes intense energy, creativity, freedom, power, vision, and courage. Fire maintains transformational and purifying powers as it gives warmth and enables life. It can also burn and destroy.

Quotes for the East:

"The earth has received the embrace of the sun and we shall see the results of that love." – Sitting Bull

"I hope you realize that every day is a fresh start for you. That every sunrise is a new chapter in your life waiting to be written." – Juansen Dizon

"The angel of the LORD *appeared to [Moses] in a flame of fire from within a bush. He looked—and the bush was ablaze with fire, but it was not being consumed."* – Exodus 3:2 New English Translation

"The greater danger for most of us lies not in setting our aim too high and falling short; but in setting our aim too low and achieving our mark." – Michelangelo

"The secret to a good morning is to watch the sunrise with an open heart." – Anthony T. Hincks

PRACTICE:

Facing to the East- *Rising into the New Day*

Feet shoulder-width apart, feeling them solidly on the ground. Roots from the bottom of my feet reach deep into the center of the earth. Hands low and relaxed. Chest open, shoulders back, face upward toward the early light.

Soaking in the morning sunshine, I acknowledge Spirit's warmth within, feeling the first rays of bathing light on my skin. A gentle flame is lit under my feet from the soft morning rays and quickly builds into a cleansing fire throughout my body. The fire kills off all the brushy top growth of weeds from the day before but does not consume me. I accept Great Spirit's smile on this day. Burning even more deeply into the core of my being, the sun's white-hot flames baptize every atom of me with light, from my toes to the top of my head.

On this new day, I begin again with a blank canvas on which anything is possible to be imagined. Basic Goodness is my core virtue. I was born at this moment in history to be here on this day. I remember my life-purpose, letting it renew my calling into the day ahead.

Beginner's Mind

The first faint light teasing itself onto the horizon is my favorite part of the day, even though on most days my eyes are still closed, and my mind and body are still asleep. For me, dawn symbolizes the simple beauty of what is called in Buddhism, *beginner's mind*, a wonderous seeing of something as if for the first time. Each day, the sunrise puts on its show regardless of audience. This is where the warrior's day begins, both metaphorically and physically. I've always been fascinated by how the daily rotation of the earth creates the appearance of the sun rising in the sky. The first rays of light have appeared to me as an invitation since I was young. I invite you to consider this moment, as your eyes glance at these words, a sunrise of sorts—a dawning of your new practice. Welcome!

Two Gifts

My mother shared just such an invitation with me many years ago. As the story goes, it was a lazy summer morning, early enough that most parents are still dozing, confident their children are also fast asleep. But not this twelve-year-old little boy. Up early, fascinated by what I saw out the window, I slipped quietly into my sleeping mother's room to rouse her out of a deep slumber. Nudging her, I insisted she follow me. Like a dutiful mom, she rubbed the sleepiness out of her eyes, and despite the litany of mischievous little boy things she may have to face cascading through her still groggy mind, she agreed to wake up. Warmly but urgently, I tugged at her hand, and she quickly followed. We landed at the picture window in the family room. She adjusted her focus from her wide-eyed son to the view out the window. In awe, we both stood gaping at the array of color filling the sky—a never-before-imagined pink, mouth-watering orange, and poetically-purple sunrise. Standing motionless, witnessing the magnificent, sacred scene before us, we were filled with a kind of spiritual validation that something divine has smiled on us.

Looking back on that moment many times since, I realize I received two precious, life-changing gifts from my mother. The first gift was the gift of listening she so effortlessly modeled. She showed me, without words how to communicate curiosity, love, and understanding. Despite whatever internal resistance she may have experienced to getting out of bed early, she didn't share any of it out loud. My urging was enough to compel her, and I felt heard, understood, and loved without even knowing it. Little did I know these skills would also become strong in me and form the heart of my professional career. It's taken me the better part of the last 30 years to learn how to listen that way myself, and every day I feel like a beginner.

The second gift I received that morning was exposure to what I believe was always a part of me, my life purpose. At the age of twelve this purpose began to take expression in my life although I didn't know what it meant at the time. Many years later, the purpose appeared before me as distinct, beautiful, and natural as that summer sunrise. Shortly after the invitation to witness the sunrise, my mother captured the pre-dawn summer morning experience in a poem. After she shared it with me, I promptly tucked it away in a file of favorite writings. Preparing for her much-too-soon memorial service fifteen years later, I remembered the poem as a timeless connection with her teaching and modeling of unconditional love. Weeping as I read it aloud at her service, I made a commitment to a life of deep listening, unconditional love, and fascination. In my own way, letting her spirit live on, through me.

I share her poem with you to set the context for the warrior's compass. It is an invitation to something beautiful inside you, to the emerging light of conscious choice, deeply connected to an ancient lineage. In the East, the warrior's day first begins with that connection to generations before and those to come.

Have you ever been invited to a sunrise?

By Dottie Parker Seagren

I have. Just this morning, right before dawn
a sleepy boy popped in with a yawn, and said,
"Come here." So I ran to see what was so
important to my twelve-year-old. My gratitude is
like the gift he gave, for he shared today's sunrise

He shared it.
He shared the coming, the beginning of his
day. He included me in the vivid hues
that promised fullness of a beautiful day.

> *I was deeply moved.*
>
> *And as I said, "thank you," it sounded hollow. Thank you never really says it all. But I meant it all new and I meant it deeply. I am grateful to have been invited to today's new day,*
>
> *today's sunrise,*
>
> *with my son.*

In the years between being reminded of this poem at my mother's memorial service in 1990 and today, my life has twisted and turned, bumped and soared, and been torn and transformed several times. With each adventure my purpose became ever clearer:

> *I am in this world to share and to be the sunrise, the new day.*

Shining a light on intrinsic potential is both easy and hard. It's easy when I get to listen to someone tell a story about something with which they're struggling. With deep compassion, I've learned to listen to those stories with my heart, holding space for what's next and what's possible. It's hard when I tangle with my inner narratives, stop listening and fall back asleep.

On-going Practice

There is great potential awaiting each of us. Yet we often give in to the relentless gravitational pull to fall back asleep. My own resistance is as persistent as the sun shining every morning. I so dearly want to wake up to catch a glimpse of the sunrise but, too often, a laundry list of reasons not to get up subtly grabs my attention. Such a slumber misses the first faint morning beams of life's stunningly simple beauty and openness. I probably miss it more days than I see it, both in reality and metaphorically. So, I've accepted the ebbs and flows of purpose as a practice, never finished.

The East is often associated with newness of spring, renewal, and a cleansing fire. It speaks to the innocence, creativity, and vision of a fresh beginning. A precious opportunity appears in the first moments of the day, moments that set the tone for everything that follows. I try to pause before getting out of bed or beginning my morning routine of reading and meditation. Simply noticing and naming that this moment is precious, then slowing down enough to notice a spectacular sunrise, listen for gifts of the day, and affirm expansion into abundance, freedom, and love, is where I try to start. It reminds me that I can, with that beginner's mind, "begin again" and connect deeply with my essential wholeness.

My intention is to bring a new light of awareness to that which is dawning in you through these pages. To let the wonder of what's possible, even in the face of chaos and uncertainty, find a foot hold. Here begins the journey into the unknown.

The Day Begins

We enter the Warrior's Compass in the East, the direction of the sunrise and illumination, where light shines onto the earth day. East represents the ability to see clearly with fresh eyes. Complexity appears only as a wisp of a cloud in the sunlight. No doubt there will be new lessons to learn. But affirming my willingness to "begin again" many times today, a new gift is opened and reopened. Too often, as I transition from being asleep to awake, thoughts flood in, like: "What day is it?" "When is my first appointment?" "Can I sleep just a little longer?" or "Do I really have to go to work when it seems like yesterday all over again?" That's assuming that more than one or two words can even be put together into a thought. Repeating the scene from the movie *Groundhog Day* when the alarm goes off at 6:00 a.m. and "I've Got You Babe" plays over and over is not the theme I choose. This day, this moment, will never repeat itself and is dearly precious. It deserves to be appreciated as unique just as today's sunrise will never happen in quite the same way ever again.

And so, I'm compelled to take some responsibility for my first few thoughts. The basis of these thoughts will likely set a tone for how the day progresses. The wee moments of transition between semi-conscious sleep and being more awake are sacred and offer the first glimpse of purposeful choice.

Intention

The first moment I realize I am awake can begin with a simple, "thank you"—both an offering of gratitude and an eager embrace of the unknown adventure ahead. When I do this regularly, my overall demeanor is more gentle, compassionate, and grateful. When I also begin in abundance, time expands, filling me with inspiration that enables me to get things done more quickly. In these waking moments I connect to a more inclusive energy and power.

Taking a few more intentional moments to myself, I set a vision each day by answering at least one of these questions:

- Listening intently, what is new about this day? How might the sun view me and what's ahead on *this* morning?
- What is drawing me forward? What might this day need from me?
- As I look at the light stretching into the day, what feeling is evoked in me? Sit with it; let it be just a feeling without an action yet.
- What were my first thoughts when I woke up today? Are they affirmative? Can I reframe them quickly into a positive statement and notice the difference?
- Is there anything from yesterday or last night's dreams that appear to already be informing this day without my consent? What do I need to let go of?
- What will make today great?

With a sense of peace, I follow my intuition and name my intention. Today I affirm: ______________________________.

For many years, I've shared my intention or affirmation via text message to my partner in life (now my wife) and accountability partner; and she texts me hers. This way, there is no forgetting, no half-baked quickly forgotten quip.

And since I do forget frequently, it's easy to go back to my text message to remember. At the end of the day, it's fun to see how that intention played out.

Despite my intention, at times the sunrise-filled sky appears only vast and empty to me. I cannot comprehend how to interface with the divine or even if a sacred celestial being exists. And still, I can embrace it *just as it is* at that moment. The Jewish philosopher Martin Buber is recorded as saying,

> *"The world is not comprehensible, but it is embraceable."*

In this embrace, I am sufficient for my day.

At other times, suffering, sorrow, and loneliness overwhelm my first few waking moments. Even though I'm up and headed into my day, I'm barely awake to its possibilities. Yet I'm beginning to see these moments also filled with a unique message. I recently heard a koan speak to this paradox. *(A koan is a paradoxical riddle, often used in Zen Buddhism to demonstrate the inadequacy of logical reasoning and rouse enlightenment.)* This one is attributed to Mizuta Masahide:

> *"My barn, having burned to the ground, I can see more completely the moon."*

The initial sorrow or loneliness with which I may awake could be an opportunity to see more of a sacred new day and embrace it.

What to Call the Sacred Divine?

Sacredness implies a spiritual quality that is beyond human invention. Regardless of tradition or theistic orientation the first moments of the day are indeed sacred. How often do I really take even a moment to make them sacred? And does that mean they have to be deep or meaningful or divine? What do I even call this experience of divinity? Is that important? As the East is about getting things in alignment for the day, it feels important to have words that resonate for me.

For many years, it was important to figure out what to call this sacred divine power. It took me most of my life to craft a unique relationship with what I grew up calling "God." Then, in a matter of several tumultuous months shortly after turning 40, leaving my career as a trader and beginning to reinvent myself, my definitions and foundations unraveled. Through the tumult—the burning down of my barn—the way was more open to see a much wider swath of the universal, my moon. How I perceived the universe changed. My entire belief system, which before stretched out to the edges of the universe as I knew it, I could now see in a still beautiful but smaller vessel before me. The container still holds many of my core beliefs, but now they are part of a much larger whole. Albert Einstein made this stark observation:

> *"The most important decision we make is whether we believe we live in a friendly or hostile universe."*

At one point in my life, this decision took on new urgency for me. Would this day be imprisoned by a hostile, skeptical force? Or was there a force conspiring with me to create the life I wanted or the life that called me? Both are fair questions. In many ways, this is a decision and commitment I get to make anew every day.

For example, I choose to see my Christian upbringing as a beautiful chapter building toward spiritual wholeness. And yet, I now view Christianity as just one of the many cards in my deck, so to speak. At one turning point, I had to un-know the "Christian God" to see my life in a larger context.

The term Great Spirit, a Native American moniker, now represents Supreme Being, or Source for me. The East is where I acknowledge Great Spirit entering my day, although like the sun, it really hasn't entered anything but my consciousness, in the holy, sacred first moments of the day. Great Spirit is unattached and unconditional. It is not out there, separate from me. If it were, my sense of aloneness would overwhelm me. So, I no longer pray *to* a divine essence. Instead, when I pray, I do so *with* the Great Spirit. Praying *with* allows me to begin the day interconnected to a larger whole. Praying *with* elicits the courage to boldly enter the day ahead. Skepticism, doubt, and fear are welcome here. They've become friends who I invite to sit around the campfire and hear what is possible for this new day. Sometimes they stay and other times they fade into the surrounding woods. Either way, because I see them as guests, they no longer hijack my system into the protected confines of diatribe and dogma.

That said, the Bible continues to inspire me as metaphor and myth. The burning bush in the story from Exodus is the basis of the kind of fire – the spirit of purifying wisdom and presence – introduced in this chapter. We are burned but not consumed by it. As Moses noticed the fantastic sight of a bush on fire, Yahweh called out to him and requested he remove his sandals, for where he was standing was sacred ground.

> *"Now Moses was keeping the flock of his father-in-law, Jethro, the priest of Midian, and he led his flock to the west side of the wilderness and came to Horeb, the mountain of God. And the angel of the Lord appeared to him in a flame of fire out of the midst of a bush. He looked, and behold, the bush was burning, yet it was not consumed. And Moses said, 'I will turn aside to see this great sight, why the bush is not burned.' When the Lord saw that he turned aside to see, God called to him out of the bush, 'Moses, Moses!' And he said, 'Here I am.' Then he said, 'Do not come near; take your sandals off your feet, for the place on which you are standing is holy ground.'"*[3]

This sacred ground is the place where each day begins. In the cleansing fire is great wisdom for today.

The Physical Element of Fire – a Reference Point

The physical element representing the East is fire. This may seem a natural complement to the blazing sun. But for me the metaphor is rooted in ecology and native landscape restoration

[3] Exodus 3:1-5 New English Translation

practices. I briefly digress here to offer my reference point for fire. You see, for years, I volunteered with a group of dedicated conservationists in my hometown of Barrington, IL, called, Citizens for Conservation. In the late 80's I started with a fascination for picking seeds in the fall, long before I knew what the plants looked like in their summer splendor. I knew many native flowers like *Monarda fistulosa* (Wild Bergamot) only by their fragrant, dried seed heads that filled my senses with smells of Earl Grey tea.

At first, we picked seeds along the train tracks spurred out into the country from downtown Chicago. Most of the Illinois prairie was turned into farmland so only a fraction of 1% of native vegetation remains, some of it along these tracks. Train maintenance crews used to burn off the vegetation next to the tracks. Non-natives couldn't withstand the annual burning, so only native plants survived. Before the train crews switched to herbicides in the late 90's, we gathered as many seeds as possible. As we picked, the elders in the group talked about the ecology of the prairies and oak groves native to the Midwest. It was then I learned about the power and presence of fire and how it shaped the Midwestern landscapes over centuries.

The rich, dark, prairie soil supports some of the most bountiful crops in the world and is known as the breadbasket of North America. I knew very little about the prairie history that allowed for soybeans and corn to be planted in abundance all over Illinois, Indiana, and Iowa. For thousands of years, fires started by lightning storms would tear across the prairies.

They became fire-tolerant communities that kept down weedy infestations of brush. Reptiles, birds, and animals thrived in the open plains created by the fires. During a wild prairie fire, the tops of the native plants burnt to a crisp and all remaining energy was sent down into the plants' very deep roots. Common natives like Compass Plant, Lead Plant and Big Bluestem have roots going down a dozen feet or more. After thousands of years, the soil became rich, deep, and enticing to those traveling west to turn the prairies into their farms so they could support their families, build communities, and eventually feed people living in far-away cities.

However, as farmland replaced the prairies, wildfires became infrequent. When fires did start, they were often put out quickly. Fire suppression became a topic of great debate among ecologists and politicians. Use of prescribed burns became more popular as a restoration technique because it favored native plants that had thousands of years of evolution behind them over the quick-growing weedy, invasive species brought in by well-meaning newcomers to the land in the late 1800's.

The drought of 1988 brought to the forefront the country's concern about fire suppression in Yellowstone National Park. The fires there were the largest in the park's history and ravaged vistas people had thought looked that way forever. The truth is, they hadn't. They were a product of millennia of regular fires that swept through, burning off the branches, weaker trees, and dead wood that littered the forest floors. When the fires were suppressed, the debris piled up so that when a fire did sweep through, it had much more fuel and therefore burned hotter than usual, and in some cases did more damage.

Within days of the Yellowstone fires burning all the fuel they could, a beautiful native plant called Fireweed sprouted up in the hardest hit parts of the park. Within 2-5 years, native wildflower populations exploded. People traveled in droves to see the once-in-a lifetime display of splendor amidst the scene of devastation. You may get the sense of why fire is so important as a cleansing agent!

The predominant tree in Yellowstone is the Lodgepole Pine. This pine often produces pinecones which won't disperse their seeds unless subjected to intense fires (known by scientists as being "serotinous"). Research of test plots established after the fires indicated the best seed dispersal occurred in areas experiencing the most severe ground fires; seed dispersal was lowest in areas that had only minor surface burns. While it remained controversial for years, fire management fundamentally changed after 1988 in parks all over the country.

Metaphorically, the renewing, catalytic nature of fire is fascinating to me. In the best of circumstances, the fires of our lives send energy down into our roots and open us up, allowing us to survive regardless of the apparent destruction on the surface. I know the ability to thrive and grow is often the result of severe tumult. Again, I am reminded that "My barn, having burned to the ground, I can see more completely the moon." Disfiguring and landscape-altering challenges may have a built-in mechanism for creating immediate growth.

Finding Opportunity in Chaos

1988 was a record year for the largest fires in the recorded history of Yellowstone National Park. It was also a record year in my fledgling commodity trading business and a new marriage at 25 years old. The Park fires happened in a drought year which affected most of the country's food crops. Drought, heat, fires, and subsequent rains created wild volatility to agricultural commodity prices. Managing that volatility became my number one job to not only survive but to leverage the opportunities created.

The open markets supported a highly capitalist system of risk transfer. Mitigating risk cost dearly during volatile markets as the entity taking on that elevated risk asked for a premium. I was trading commodity options on one of the country's largest crops: soybeans and its derivatives, soybean meal, and soybean oil. Options prices are determined by a complex mathematical formula that has a significant subjective input called "volatility." As uncertainty ruled the markets, the difference between the bid and ask price of the options widened. That meant increased risk and opportunity for profit if one kept his wits about him and learned what risk management really entailed. I learned to fail and recover quickly, again and again! It turned out to be the most profitable year of my 20-year trading career, financially and in the abundance of life lessons, both of which honed my character. Along the way, I found an inner calm that serves me to this day.

Fire, chaos, opportunity, calm. Such a powerful combination for warriorship. There is no mistake that the beginning of the day in the East is associated with fire as the primal energy that keeps us alive. Fire is dangerous and can be catastrophic if not managed well. The warrior's morning path is about leaning into all that potential and embracing it with deep awareness and kindness. That doesn't happen overnight. So, setting a powerful vision and moving with purpose is part of the practice every day.

Vision, Purpose and Eldership

My favorite example of a powerful vision is from Black Elk, the Oglala Lakota Sioux medicine man, when he was just nine years old. While severely ill and unresponsive over several days he received a vision of visiting his grandfathers in the four cardinal directions, each with a specific teaching. When he finally told Black Road, an elder medicine man about his vision in detail when he was seventeen, he recalled the message:

> *"Behold this day, for it is yours to make."*

I've often thought of this upon waking in the morning. At that moment, the day is a blank canvas and mine to create.

We create from the sacred messages we receive when we get quiet enough to listen. With practice, each day's vision begins to correspond with the greater vision or purpose set before us.

Many books have been written on finding one's purpose. In my search for how to articulate what I felt within me, I found a process started by Tim Kelly that has evolved into the True Purpose Institute. What resonated with me most in his process was developing a co-active relationship with one's Trusted Source. People define this source differently depending on their religious views, cultural traditions, and country of origin. For me, Trusted Source, Great Spirit, comes to speak through a Wisdom Circle of elders. These are people in my life who have graciously mentored and called me forth, and teachers with whom I studied either personally or through reading their published works. Periodically, characters who I have never met appear to me to speak their wisdom.

Black Elk is a key member of my Wisdom Circle and has spoken several times. A white-clad warrior goddess astride her white horse speaks infrequently. Thich Nhat Hahn, the Zen Buddhist monk, steps in from time to time as do my mother and father. This may seem fanciful or romantic. But dream states often feel this way. I side with Black Elk's observation,

"Sometimes dreams are wiser than waking."

In my morning thoughts, my elders are very awake and very wise. They encourage me to be a thought-leader and take responsibility for the impact I have on my world.

The Wisdom Circle gives me input as I ask for it and stay connected to its essence. Most often, this happens through an active dialogue process pioneered by Carl Jung. Journaling my queries, I receive the answers I need. Through this process, I confirmed my purpose in the world as described by Tim Kelly and the True Purpose Institute. He taught me that purpose is a function of Essence, Blessing, and Mission. That made it much more accessible. My Essence is that of a sunrise. My Blessing is to claim the true self. My Mission is to work with leaders who use business as a force for good.

For many years, I would reconnect with the elders in my Wisdom Circle every Sunday evening. Now, sometimes many months go by without an intentional, specific connection, but these elders are always with me. They are interconnected with my best self, and I can tap into their wisdom any time.

Arnold Mindell, another of my influential teachers, contrasts eldership with leadership in his book *Sitting in the Fire.* Here he provokes a very specific kind of elder in action and practice which is akin to the elders in my Wisdom Circle. He says:

- The leader follows *Roberts Rules of Order;* the elder obeys the spirit.
- The leader seeks a majority; the elder stands for everyone.

- The leader sees trouble and tries to stop it; the elder sees the troublemaker as a possible teacher.
- The leader strives to be honest; the elder sees the truth in everything.
- The democratic leader supports democracy; the elder does this too but also listens to dictators and ghosts.
- Leaders try to be better at their jobs; elders try to get others to become elders.
- Leaders try to be wise; elders have no mind of their own—they follow the events of nature.
- The leader knows; the elder learns.
- The leader needs a strategy; the elder studies the moment.
- The leader follows a plan; the elder honors a direction of a mysterious and unknown river.

This distinction isn't meant to demean leaders. Rather, as conscious leaders become compassionately present, without attachment and in touch with a larger sense of the whole, their eldership emerges. It is this voice of eldership I listen for when I connect with my Wisdom Circle to reconfirm my purpose and direction. It is the voice I listen for in the morning as the sun rises in the East.

A beautiful connection with Spirit and the East confirms that I do indeed have a purpose in the world. Remembering this allows me to act it out anew each day without judgment. My purpose is a calling forth and a witnessing of the human spirit. It is as native to us as breathing and becomes apparent as we are willing to really listen. I always had some sense of who I was at my core and went through many iterations of expressing it, and I sense that as I grow older (or elder as I understand many native Americans say) there will be further refinement and remembering.

When I let the morning sunshine soak through me, it connects with Great Spirit, which remembers my purpose without fail. I've learned that it's helpful to write out this purpose almost daily. Remembering who I am is both an inspiration and an enormity that scares me. That's when I know I'm in the right place to listen deeply to the words. My purpose, in its present form, is expressed this way:

> *I am the rock-star/serenity sunrise that claims the true, magnificent self in service of wholeness, unconditional love, and creative possibility. As a spiritual warrior, I pledge to open my heart and speak my truth.*

Knowing my purpose is vital to dealing with the complexity of today. Whatever storms may come, this purpose serves as a beacon to correct my course and calm my thoughts. To know a purpose is like riding on a train while lost in thought elsewhere—it just keeps on moving you forward.

Necessary Tension between Vision and Current Reality

Having a vision and a purpose is vital to my getting out of bed in the morning. But when it's disconnected from what is currently happening, I get lost and lose faith. That's a problem! For a clue on how to deal with this paradox, I turned to Jim Collins and his book *Good to Great*. He tells the story of Admiral James Stockdale, the senior most naval officer held captive in Vietnam. He survived being regularly tortured and denied medical attention for 7 ½ years. Many of his colleagues died in while in captivity. Stockdale shared his coping strategy with Collins in contrast with those who perished. He said,

> *"I never doubted not only that I would get out, but also that I would prevail in the end and turn the experience into the defining event of my life, which, in retrospect, I would not trade."*

He goes on to share his most important lesson:

> *"You must never confuse faith that you will prevail in the end – which you can never afford to lose – with the discipline to confront the most brutal facts of your current reality, whatever they might be."*

Collins called this the "Stockdale Paradox." With a powerful purpose must also come a sense of what is ahead today, even if it is not a life-or-death choice. What are the brutal facts of today? Are those facts known in detail? What is the vision that will help today be one of survival?

Both vision and current reality meet in creative tension, says Robert Fritz in *The Path of Least Resistance*. He uses the term "productive flourishing" when these same two things are clearly known. The two are connected by energy that pulls them closer as if bound by a rubber band. Creative tension is the structure that energizes the changes both in thought and action that need to take place to achieve the vision.

Fritz says, however, that problems can arise when we relieve the pent-up tension between current reality and our vision. As a means of easing the tension we lower our vision, and come close to Michelangelo's saying,

> *"The greater danger for most of us lies not in setting our aim too high and falling short; but in setting our aim too low and achieving our mark."*

The process of connecting energetically with your vision and purpose each day is a way to aim much higher and see what's possible. While also confronting what's ahead, as suggested by Stockdale and Fritz, the day begins to take its full shape. The practice is to stay with the energy of "productive flourishing" just a little bit longer each day.

A Very Personal Story

Before ending our time in the East, I'd like to share a very personal story to give you an example of how this morning practice began. It illustrates why the cleansing fire is a required starting place for the new day and how it can bring to the surface latent longing.

In late 2003, I had been married for 15 years and had two children. My mortgage was paid off, my savings accounts were growing, and life was pretty good on the surface. Over 11 years I created a dream job-sharing arrangement with my father in which I worked in the business every other month. During the off months, I had time to respond to calls for healing that had slowly started to come in more frequently, travel with my family and have time to stay in shape while doing projects around the house.

With all that, my business partnership with my father disintegrated over a difference of opinion on the direction of the business that was brewing for several years. I decided to leave. It was a major jolt to my well-crafted system. Suddenly I had a lot more time to figure out how to reinvent myself. My soul searching began in earnest to discover who I was supposed to be in the world, how I was being called into a unique purpose, and how I would make a living to continue supporting my family. My business success to that point meant that I had a financial safety net that would help support my family for at least several years while my reinvention gained traction.

Like the searing hot fire needed to release the seeds inside lodgepole pinecones, this experience cracked me wide open, releasing something stored inside me for years, untapped. New growth was certain, but the impact of the fires was still unknown. The internal work of purifying and refining was finally ready to be tested real time.

I was pretty headstrong when it came to following my new-found path and this took a toll on my relationships with my father, my siblings, and my marriage. My father and I so disagreed on things we didn't talk for 3 ½ years. I was no longer the same successful financial provider to my family. Exploring what it meant to provide spiritual nourishment wasn't paying too many bills, and yet I knew in my deepest soul, the necessity of this growth track.

Like any personal growth, it is just that, personal. I tried to share what I was learning with others, but many times I didn't know how to find words to describe the cellular reorganization of my core being. I pursued my growth with abandon, mostly on my own. How do you reconcile your soul's longing for expression with needs right in front of you? I was experiencing the creative tension model in real-time. Tension becomes stress that needs relief by either letting go of the vision or ignoring the current reality. At the time, I couldn't hold both. That was one of the key life-lessons I had to learn by failing.

To hold the stress of my soul-searching and exploration, pushing edges and finding new, purposeful work, my most important relationships would need incredible gentleness, forgiveness, and vulnerability. But that's not what happened. It took nearly four years to have an opening conversation with my father and another two or three to begin healing. Gratefully, today we are good friends, can laugh and joke together (as long as we don't discuss the past!), and have a deep love for each other. What failed as a business partnership found common ground on being father and son. I'm grateful to my father for offering me the opportunity to learn real, lasting forgiveness and unselfish generosity despite receiving nothing in return, something my father did for so many others, even when others advised him to stop giving.

As I continued exploring who I was meant to be in this new chapter of my life, I went through many iterations of new identities. I built my healing practice, took an advocacy position within my church, and built a conflict resolution and mediation practice. I began supporting organization's leadership teams through communication difficulties and taking increasing calls for healing. That morphed into a leadership coaching practice that had a spiritual element of support to every interaction. I became a learning junkie, taking every coaching, leadership and systems coaching certification class I could. It felt like I had finally found a way to bring together my healing practice, business experience and calling to be a guide for others. I was finally finding my true purposeful calling.

Unfortunately, my marriage didn't fare so well. Initially a support system, doubt crept in about my ability to be a support to my family. That turned into resentment. My commitment to the marriage waned when we hit a major rough spot. We couldn't find a way get through on the same page despite counselor and coaching support.

Fast forward a few years, through a separation and then a divorce, when the kids were just entering their college years. I found myself living alone for the first time in nearly 25 years. I'd often wake up during the wee hours of the morning in a slight panic about what had happened. How did I get here? This was not part of my long-term plan. I was following my innermost heart and it was simultaneously broken open. Some nights I'd stay awake for hours spinning things through my weary mind battling between being excruciatingly hard on myself and training my ear to listen to my heart and soul. Creative tension at 3am is often dark and lonely.

In the light of day, I could see that I was on an amazing journey of claiming wholeness, love, and connection. A relationship with a fellow traveler grew into a beautiful partnership of witnessing and reassurance, especially during the dark times. Life's messy parts were held as natural and all part of who we are – a lesson I desperately needed to learn. There was no crying over spilled milk here! Our love was one known for centuries and lifetimes. While we lived a thousand miles apart, our kindred spirits were never separate. Today, we are married and have built a solid foundation of expanded family, including all our combined children and the clients we serve.

It was during these years I found this practice of greeting the sunrise every morning with an open mind to the new day. Fire and sun seemed to fit perfectly together as a profound way to begin the day afresh. Letting the metaphorical fires burn slowly at first, and then with practice letting them get hotter and hotter, I let the cleansing flames work me over. What I found was that they started "top-killing" my mental struggles and sending my energy deep into my body. The flames taught me to find a gentle way of letting go of my attachments to how things were supposed to be and begin again each day.

Of course, this didn't happen all at once. Like any practice, it continued to unfold in uneven stages. To this day, my practice still requires great humility, vulnerability, and trust. As I slowly let go of the harsh mental berating and inner-turmoil, and eventually even the residue from a night of wrestling, each morning becomes truly a begin-again moment—fresh, restored, and cleansed. Gentleness to myself is an absolute prerequisite.

The Great Eastern Sun

One integral learning during this time of upheaval in my life was of the Buddhist idea of the Great Eastern Sun, and its corresponding value of Basic Goodness, the most basic human virtue. The vision of the Great Eastern Sun is that no human being is a lost cause. They are the expression of true human goodness, based not on arrogance and aggression, but gentleness and openness. East represents the dawning of wakefulness. By deeply appreciating first our own, and then everyone's inherent brilliance, we wake to be a natural a source of radiant light. From that recognition, my sense of dignity arises, and this is where I find my work in the world. Beginning the day with a bow to my innate goodness allows intentions to take root, visions to be seen and purpose to be lived.

This ends the first cardinal direction, the East, the home of the rising sun. Most mornings I spend the greater portion of my compass time here, before moving on to the other directions. It is in the East that I connect deeply with my best self, reaffirm my vision, and affirm a positive intention to guide me through the day. Just as the sun continues to rise on the horizon from my earthly view as the day commences, it is time to move on to the next direction and the wisdom of the first Owl, Unconditional Love.

SOUTHEAST

Feeling Unconditional Love, Compassion and Gentleness

Quotes for the Southeast:

"Unconditional love is the beautiful hoped-for impossibility, and yet we could not fully understand the nature of our helplessness without looking through the lens of that hoped for perfection." – David Whyte

"We cultivate love when we allow our most vulnerable and powerful selves to be deeply seen and known, and when we honor the spiritual connection that grows from that offering with trust, respect, kindness and affection." – Brené Brown

"Ring the bells that still can ring
Forget your perfect offering
There is a crack, a crack in everything
That's how the light gets in." – Leonard Cohen (Anthem)

PRACTICE:
Facing toward the Southeast - *Feeling unconditional love, compassion, and gentleness*

Standing with arms outstretched, palms facing the sky, and eyes gently closed; feeling a warm, orange-hued liquid filling up the body from the toes upward, pouring out the top of the head, then back down through the fingers, and the toes, overflowing into the whole room, the house, the neighborhood, the community, down every street and into every river, expanding to the whole country, across oceans, around the world and with increasing pace, into all space ... the stars, the universe and beyond.

I am here to be a vessel of radiance – to give unselfishly and to love unconditionally. This starts with all that is good and flows through all of me: the beautiful, the shameful, the forgiven, the slightly awkward, the delightfully brilliant, and the ugly. All parts of me are included. Waves of unconditional love ripple outward to loved ones and family, then out to close friends, then colleagues, neighbors, and finally strangers around the world, touching every heart. I pause on each person, feeling loving kindness and compassion.

May you all be healthy. May you all find gentleness in your suffering. May you all be resilient and comforted. May you all be happy.

The Owls Arrive

In the Southeast the first Owl makes its entrance, representing Unconditional Love. I capitalize these words here to indicate they are in some mystical sense, a manifestation of the divine. Immediately upon recognizing the sunrise, my vision, and who I choose to be in this day, this Owl comes with the reminder to be gentle and kind, connecting me with my innate capacity for deep, Unconditional Love. This chapter is short, but the one hardest to master for me – indeed, Love is a journey rather than a destination. When I notice judgments about myself hijacking the day, it's time to come back to this place. It's time to learn how to fall in love with myself and all my imperfections. Can you take a moment or an hour today, to fall in love with yourself? What might be available if you did? What is it you most appreciate about yourself right now? Spend as much time here as you need, especially underscoring love for the not-so-pretty parts of yourself. This is the first Owl's work—to gently and patiently remind us to let compassion and love radiate inward so that it may then radiate outward.

Putting Owls in Context

I grew up taking a lot of art classes. It's likely that since my mom was an art major in college it was natural to have paint, clay, and sketch pads around the house. But I was also naturally drawn to expressing myself through what my hands created from what I saw in my mind's eye. My mom's love of art and all things amusing infused my childhood perspective and formed in me a deep appreciation for color, pattern, and design. I thought all kids grew up appreciating artistic beautiful design and saw deliciously whimsical faces in the window and door patterns on every house, tree bark, and pile of scattered papers on the floor. I think my mom considered the most complete work of art to be either the owl or the cat. Both have large cartoonish eyes and playful facial expressions. The owl's wizened eyes hide its surgically precise hunting ability. And its ears! Horn-like tufts of feathers or large discs take up most of its face, while its serrated-edged feathers carry it silently, eerily through the air.

And so, in my childhood home, there was an ever-growing collection of figurines, paintings, lunchboxes, and post cards. Anything that had an owl on it was collectible. For my siblings and me, owls and my mom were intricately connected. Ever since her passing in 1990, we all note owl sightings as a reminder of her many wonderful qualities—the most inspiring of which was her demonstrable unconditional love.

I'll never forget one story of her expression of that unbounded kindness. One day a friend of hers came over to chat. She brought with her a very curious little boy who cruised through the house to inspect every corner. When he found her owl figurine collection, he picked up each one with interest. Unfortunately, he bumped into the table on which the owls were perched, and one fell to the floor with a crash. The boy's mother ran to find out what happened and was horrified to find one of the little sculptures in pieces on the floor and her sheepish son biting his tongue and grimacing. They brought the shards to my mom with an apology and her reply still resonates deeply in my heart, even though I wasn't there that day. She reportedly said, "Of course I forgive you, but there is something I want you to do for me. At some point in your life, someone will break or harm something that is very dear to you and you're going to have the opportunity to forgive them unconditionally, from your heart." And with that, a seed of beautifully gentle and deep, unconditional love was planted in that little boy for the rest of his life. This is the standard she set for me as well: love without expectation of getting direct benefit in return as the most important aspect of love.

This is the link between the first owl and unconditional love. The owl's appearance here in the Warrior's Compass is important. For if I cannot first love all parts of myself with full acceptance, very little "right" action and certainly very little truly selfless loving will follow. Accepting the unknown and unappreciated in myself is requisite to accepting the mystery of life around me.

What's in a Name?

A bit more context for how owls became important to me personally and on a deeply spiritual level is significant to share here. The name "*Three Owls*" was given to me by nature itself, as in the Native American tradition. Naming traditions, while varying greatly from tribe to tribe, are descriptive names like, Little Black Eyes or High Backbone. They can describe a role like She Who Takes the Babies (a midwife) or be drawn from nature, like Sitting Bull, Little Thunder and Red Cloud. A name given to a baby would change with adulthood, and a person could have several names over a lifetime. Native American names were often chosen to mark major events in life and could change with new achievements, experiences, and accomplishments. Names also included totem animals, which served as a spirit guide, sacred object, or symbol of a tribe, clan, family or individual. In shamanism, an animal totem is meant to be a representation of the traits and skills that an individual is supposed to learn, acquire, or embody. Though people may identify with different animal guides throughout their lifetimes, it is this one totem animal that acts as the foremost guardian spirit. Native American names often had very personal and sacred meanings and were used only in ceremonial circles, not for ordinary address.

For most of my life, especially since my mom's passing, owls showed up during significant beginnings and endings and were clearly a sacred "totem" for me. So, the name *Three Owls* was very natural for me to receive. There are many stories and myths around the receiving of a Native American name. What I most appreciate is that in some way these names find us. Some believe that native ancestors who have gone before us look for opportunities to have us earn our spirit name. I believe that I have "remembered" my ceremonial, inner guide's name as a powerful storyteller. It is the inner voice of best self and future self and the spirit that speaks the reality of what is ultimately true about mankind, that he is naturally whole and came complete with everything he needs to live his life fully and at one with all beings. It is what is possible for us despite our self-limiting beliefs, doubts, and fears.

My Name Arrives

Around my mid-40s, I sensed that I was entering the second half of my life. Wanting to honor this transition, I asked one of my teachers, Pat Carrington-House, to help create a ceremony for me. The ceremony he suggested and we co-created, involved spending as many days as would be needed, by myself on my land in the Sandhills region of central Nebraska—a half-section of rich, sandy bottom land spanning one mile of the Middle Loup River.

First, I needed to find the right location. As I walked the land, I held an openness to all the inputs happening around me: birds, grasses, grasshoppers, wind, trees … and a sort of third-ear open to the energy that would call me. A sandy ridge surrounded by Cedar and Cottonwood trees and Sand Blue-stem grasses was just the spot, confirmed by a force beyond me that said, “Yes, this is the place.” I cleared the spot of as many Sandbur Weeds as I could (an obnoxious, thorny little grass seed that has very sharp needles and finds its way into just about everything). Next, I set about identifying the cardinal directions and collecting enough firewood to last me for several days.

The idea was to get completely immersed in nothing but my journey of life to this point: dreaming about it, writing about it, and contemplating it without interruption until it was ready to be released, in as many days as that might take. On the first morning, with my fire burning, I set about dividing my life into a series of seven-year chapters and writing all the significant events, pains, joys, relationships, successes, and failures I could remember from each. I sat in the cardinal directions of the circle and considered each chapter from the angle of the gift from that direction, in the manner offered by Angeles Arriens' book, *The Fourfold Way: Walking the Paths of the Warrior, Teacher, Healer and Visionary.* As I finished each seven-year chapter of my life, I read the story of that section aloud to the fire, releasing it into the heat and smoke that rose into the sky.

On the second morning, I took a long walk as I did each day, armed only with my binoculars and a canteen of fresh water. Passing a familiar section of cottonwood trees, I was startled to notice three large birds flushing from their overnight perch. Confirming with my binoculars, these birds were three owls, an unusual sight given that owls are normally solitary creatures. Likely, it was a parent with two juveniles who, while able to fly, hadn't left the security and providing of their doting parent.

Having such an affinity to owls for so much of my life, it wasn't surprising to take special notice of these birds. Upon returning to my sacred circle later that morning, I put the question out to the fire, the sun, and the universe: "What is the significance of this sighting?" Answering very soon after my asking, as a voice from the whispering trees, was a clear,

"YOU ARE *THREE OWLS* – THIS IS YOUR NAME." Over the coming days as I read through and spoke my stories out loud, a gift from each owl became very clear.

The first owl's gift was from my maternal ancestry, the gift of Unconditional Love. The second owl's gift (she will appear in the Northwest) was the gift of freedom to try new things and fail and forgiveness when those failures hurt other people. The third owl's gift was from the more awake part of my adult nature, the gift of holding everything as an interconnected whole, as one (she will appear in the Northeast). And thus, I humbly and heartily accepted my new name *Three Owls*. The essence of these beautiful creatures began to speak through the sacred compass by way of the "life-perspective" directions in the Southeast, Northwest, and Northeast.

Over the following days, I began to see all my stories clustered around these three elements. This was no coincidence. Mother Nature had spoken her message to me of what was deeply important in my life. After three and half days I knew my ceremony was complete and I could go home to my family and life with a new calling—and a turbulence that tested me to the core.

Learning Compassion and Unconditional Love

Unconditional Love necessarily demands compassion. That compassion starts with something divine and flows through me directly to those parts of myself that are deemed unworthy, ugly, shameful, or embarrassing. I often wonder if I can love my inner darkness and nightmares just as much as I love my smile and my best talents, and if so, how? Every scar both internal and external is evidence that I have survived, healed, and have a unique story to tell.

To hold this level of compassion, I'm finding that what's most needed is a deep, honest, and oh-so-tender gentleness. I cannot get to self-love without a deep and enduring gentleness. I spent most of my life being quite proud of being tough on myself. I figured this was the reason I was successful in sports, business, and most things I put my mind to; I had a plan and executed on it, doing whatever was needed. Refocus! Try harder! Start again! Get back in the saddle!

Those commands, while still helpful at times and still relevant, no longer get to include a whip. They come with gentleness and kindness. Does that sound soft and gooey? It might; it sure would have to me a decade ago. But I find being gentle, while more difficult, is an even more effective pathway to Unconditional Love.

On one of the walls in my home, I have a framed quote that was beautifully written in calligraphy by my friend and amazing artist, Barbara Bash. It reminds me every time I walk up the stairs just how important, and difficult, it is to be gentle with myself. The saying reads:

"Behind the gentleness is always discipline"

I think it can also read the other way: *Behind the discipline is always gentleness.* In a book about warriors, what place is there for gentleness? I believe wholeheartedly that without it, a warrior is just a fighter. This is where the distinction is for me: a warrior knows how to be both gentle and fierce. The warrior uses compassion and insight as his weapons. While the fighter seeks to destroy, the warrior seeks to uplift and restore. This is the only way I can see any way into the unknown of our current world circumstances.

From a human sense, I'm not sure truly *Unconditional* Love is possible. I think we're wired to put certain conditions on things as a way of remaining safe. But we're not just human beings! I'm able to consider an unconditioned love by also being a fully spiritual being. This level of love requires both an outflow directly from Spirit and an honest acceptance of my human imperfections. Paradox often enters the day bright and early.

Self-Love Ripples Outward

From the paradox of holding gentleness and fierceness, my thought can expand into possibility. After loving all parts of me, I move to those closest to me and out from there to loved ones and friends, other people I know, and those I will never meet. May Love flow out to each one. Every person struggling today may be blessed by this radiance of Unconditional Love.

Compassion also includes all the animals who provide food for their offspring, migrate north and south, evolve, and go extinct. Love flows to every blade of grass, every insect, every photosynthetic leaf, and every wisp of wind, cloud, and drop of rain. Even when my own attempt at feeling and expressing Unconditional Love does not specifically include each element of life, its force continues outward without interruption and without condition. This outward flow of Unconditional Love necessarily includes those I'm at odds with and those I don't agree with. Richard Rohr, in one of his daily meditations sent from his *Center for Action and Contemplation*, said:

> *"If you want to find God, then honor God within you, and you will always see God beyond you. For it is only God in you who knows where and how to look for God.*
>
> *When you honor and accept the divine image within yourself, you cannot help but see it in everybody else, too, and you know it is just as undeserved and unmerited as it is in you. I call this the 'Principle of Likeness.' From this frame you stop judging and start loving unconditionally, without asking whether someone is worthy or not. The breakthrough occurs at once, although the realization deepens and takes on greater conviction over time."*

To me this is such a beautiful description of how Spirit informs the *unconditional* part of love. It doesn't define *what* is loved.

Love can be a tricky word to use in the context of daily life because it's considered soft and touchy-feely. And yet, without it as the outward flow from Spirit, life would not exist. This is freeing for the thought leader who considers her quest to be an outpouring of love for life itself. I am no longer afraid or withholding in my use of this word and concept. I am no longer concerned if it strikes someone as soft or not allowed in the world of business transactions and corporate strategy. Without it, those actions lack meaning, dignity, and depth.

Unconditional Love rippling outward offers ease and safety to conflict, chaos, and complexity. To imagine entering each day on a path already traversed by Love, creates less friction, allows for greater impact, and requires me to take less responsibility, or rather less of a false sense of responsibility for my impact. It gives me full permission to be my authentic self.

Being Three Owls in the World

I offer two stories:

First in a business context: I frequently facilitate roundtables of business leaders as part of my work as a Vistage Chair. I'm the leaders' guide, helping to enhance their lives and increase their effectiveness. When I consider the gravity of being one of the "few who guide the many," the weight can sometimes seem overwhelming. I might make a misstep, say the wrong thing, or somehow have a hidden agenda to want something more for them than they want for themselves. But when I begin the day with letting a force for good pave the way, my work becomes easier. I am not there to do anything but hold them in a way that nobody else does – as wholly loved, complete, and worthy.

I begin to listen differently when I come from a place of love and compassion. I let go of my wanting and my hopes and fears, and learn just to be present, open, and curious. After these conversations, all I want is for the people around the table to feel loved. Starting my day with Unconditional Love opens the door for me to be an open conduit for divine presence. Without needing to name it out loud for my clients, this is the inspiration of Three Owls showing up in my working relationships with senior leaders.

Second, from a more personal experience: My first trip to China in 2005 included visiting many Buddhist monasteries. One special visit allowed my family members to split up, wander at our own pace, and take in the scents and sounds. At one point, I walked by a very small, gentle-looking monk and we shared a shy smile. In a moment, something touched my heart deeply. As I paused a second longer to take in the feeling of being seen for who I really am, the man handed me a simple string of beads. Holding out my hand, he slipped them on my wrist, bowed slightly, and then with smiling eyes meeting mine, bowed again. It was a special moment. I walked on through the monastery with a warmed heart and a slightly lighter step.

Upon returning to our meeting spot with our young Tibetan guide, I must have had a gentle smile on my face. He noticed the bracelet right away and asked eagerly "Do you know what that means?" Thinking I should have a well-thought-out answer, I paused. After a few moments, I muttered something like, "Not really, but it feels right." He smiled gently and said something that 15 years later I can remember like it was yesterday. "It means you've committed to a life of compassion." Every time I think of those words, I get slightly choked up and I look at my wrist to appreciate the beads I still wear as a reminder. While the original sandalwood string fell apart years ago, I have many replacements that hold the same personal message: *I have committed to a life of compassion.*

Several months before, while struggling with my relationship with my father, I had committed to finding a compassionate way to be with him in my mind. I knew that somehow the resolution could only come from that place. But in this moment, someone who didn't know me, who lived his life in full commitment to compassion, saw me and loved me for who I was right then. Could I commit to that kind of living? I knew it was a question I could live into during the coming months, and now years. I now have the words for what this commitment meant: it is my moment-by-moment opportunity to be Three Owls in the world.

I ask myself every time I'm confronted with news reports of climate catastrophes, political divides, and human atrocities: Is my heart big enough and strong enough to reach those places? Where is my compassion when I'd rather not pay attention to those things happening far away? Why am I indifferent sometimes? In those humbling moments I'm learning to accept the Love – Universal and Unconditional – that is already there. When my heart opens just a smidge more, I align with that truth. It is known on a different plane, one that supersedes and exists within the unknown of the human world. Sometimes that is enough to find peace in my heart. Sometimes my heart breaks for my inability to send enough love out to those places.

Leonard Cohen's words from his song *Anthem*, ring true: *"Forget your perfect offering/ There is a crack, a crack in everything/ That's how the light gets in."* Indeed, my humbling broken-openness, is where the light of compassion enters my heart and is arranged to radiate outward to others.

I'm also learning to accept that being broken-open is part of the work of Unconditional Love. I'm told there is always an imperfection deliberately woven into the corner of Navajo rugs. From the untrained eye, it looks flawless. Then there's the "mistake" put there on purpose because they say that's where the Spirit moves in and out of the rug. I'm ok with being imperfect, as it were – wounded and scarred. Perhaps that's just how I was designed so the spirit of Love could move through me. The scars tell a beautiful story of healing, resilience, and pain. They represent the times I learned to love myself and others more. The light of Unconditional Love will find its way in you as well. Don't be surprised to find it in the most unexpected places.

And so, the Owl of Unconditional Love has done her work for today. The other two Owls will appear in the Northwest and the Northeast. Unconditional Love has reminded me that we have a limitless capacity for compassion. Beginning with myself and radiating outward, I can hold everyone who comes into my thoughts with kindness and warmth. I'm ready to move to the South, filled full and fulfilled.

SOUTH

Opening the Feminine Heart

ELEMENT: ***Water:*** Water is constantly flowing, even if only just beneath the surface. It has a cleansing power and is symbolic of fluidity, purification, regeneration, fertility, receiving and is life-giving.

Quotes for the South:

"Pay attention to what makes you feel most at home, grounded, and centered, whether it's a location, person, activity or thing. Find ways to bring more of those things, places, and people into your life on a regular basis. Go to places that feel like home, connect with those that bring you back to yourself, and curate items that root you in your truth." – Stephenie Zamora

"The Muses are essential stewards and initiators of the creative healthy feminine principle – that which beautifies, contains, nurtures, deepens and remains still and that which responds to people and things without any will to use or manipulate them." – Angeles Arrien

"Whither shall I go from thy spirit? Or whither shall I flee from thy presence? If I ascend up into heaven, thou art there: if I make my bed in hell, behold thou are there. If I take the wings of the morning and dwell in the uttermost parts of the sea; even there shall thy hand lead me, and thy right hand shall hold me. If I say surely darkness shall cover me, even the night shall me light about me. Yea, the darkness hideth not from thee; but the night shineth as the day: the darkness and the light are both alike to thee. For thou hast possessed my reins: thou hast covered me in my mother's womb." – Psalms 139 KJV

"To touch the earth is to move in harmony with nature." – Oglala Sioux

PRACTICE:

Facing to the South - *Opening the Feminine Heart*

Feel the moisture all the way from the tropics wafting northward. Conspiring with the skies overhead to bring a warm rain that falls gently on my head, washes down my shoulders and arms, legs, and feet, dripping off my fingertips and out my toes, taking with it any residue of ash from the flames of the East. Drenched in these warm waters I am bathed by a source outside myself. The warmth creates a kind of Teflon mantle whereby anything that would attempt to attach itself to me (self-doubt, criticism, blame, low self-esteem, etc.) doesn't stick - it simply washes away.

Cleansed, I hear a sweet, gentle voice, saying: May all my words be spoken from love, encouragement, and empathy, mending what needs mending and giving balm to a fearful and lonely world. I feel empathy for all of life, natural and human.

I give myself to this day wholeheartedly – no reserve for fear, scarcity, or uncertainty. As a healer, I love and heal myself first. Baptized clean and free to give birth to a new day with clarity, inspiration and fresh energy, the waters flowing away from my feet grow into rivers and lakes and reservoirs of healing.

Home Base

The south embodies all the finest qualities of home. For me this evokes the feminine elements of love, warmth, nurturing and a caring attitude toward others. This is the place you come back to when you need to find solid ground and safety. It feels like falling into your mother's arms when you're scared and don't know what to do next. I've always wondered why this feels like mothering rather than fathering. It certainly has elements of both, but what I'm finding is that the mothering must necessarily come first.

Beginning with feminine qualities is key to this model – in fact I think it's vital to life itself. If you think about it, life is physically conceived by the coming together of both male and female cells. And yet, gestation in most species happens within the female. We are literally forged and developed within our mothers. What was the divine purpose that creation begins with the feminine?

It makes intuitive sense that a newborn being, whether animal or human is forged in traditional feminine qualities such as caring connection, heart, warmth, creativity, beauty, nurturing, empathy, patience, inclusion, vulnerability, listening, harmony, and trust. In the cradle of these attributes, we are born. Shouldn't my thoughts and actions begin in the same place? This is why warriorship, in this compass gets grounded on home base – in the feminine.

Courage and bravery, qualities traditionally associated with warriorship are most effective when they are deeply rooted in and begin with empathy and gentleness. Notice what happens in you when you read this... home base begins with empathy and *grows into* bravery – not the other way around. If the masculine qualities of determination, drive, assertiveness, stability, independence, reason, and focus are strong in you, how does that sit with you? If you're like me, I suspect two things happen. First, a tough-guy inner critic weighs in with advance warning not to risk being seen as weak or too touchy-feely. Second, somewhere deep inside, there is a knowing native truth that is acknowledged. Both are normal and both are needed. But, too often masculine pride marginalizes the second instinct, especially in men.

Of course, it's normal to be skeptical. We are hard-wired to keep ourselves alive. There is plenty of neuroscience available to the layman delineating our two brains: first, our reptilian, "old" brain, based in the amygdala that has no capacity for language and only knows fight, flight or freeze; and second, our pre-frontal cortex, "new" brain where rational thinking and language is formed. Sometimes it is sheer determination and quick thinking that hears the proverbial rustling in the bushes and grabs a spear in case it is indeed a lion stalking his dinner.

That's what I'd call the masculine, street fighter – sinewy and taught. But we are also evolved to take a second look, inviting curiosity. That's what I consider the feminine lioness – cunning and wise. The warrior's shield and spear are at the ready, no doubt. But along with them, come insight and compassion, the vital weapons for today's warrior. Rarely is the next action or word out of my mouth a matter of life or death.

Most of life will go on after the next few minutes! And so too, in conversations, context of building relationship and rapport are more important to establish before getting to content and action plans. The Center for Right Relationship (CRR Global) calls this Relationship Systems Intelligence. Like emotional intelligence it is widely known as a key ingredient for effective business leadership. Building one's ability to ascertain the strengths, opportunities, threats, and weaknesses of any given relationship is vital to deeper connection with others. It is like a muscle that can both be strengthened and can atrophy when not used.

Compassion, empathy, gentleness, and insight are fierce allies and are not soft. While we traditionally think of them as soft skills, it's time to consider them as *vital* skills, not at all soft and fluffy. This is home base.

A quick example: Imagine you're standing in line to board a flight. The skies are clear, and the flags are barely waving. Then a notice comes over the PA system that your flight is delayed by 4 hours due to weather at your location. The avalanche of thoughts that begins to swirl tend to build intensity and anxiety quickly. Maybe a connecting flight or an important meeting will be missed. For me, at that moment, finding my home base is important before words begin to come out of my mouth. When I can take a deep breath, find even a scrap of gentleness, most often my experience flows more smoothly, and I don't say things I might later regret. This is why it is so important to have warriorship begin in the feminine domain.

Physical Discipline

In the south, first thing in the morning, gently birthing the new day into being, is also the discipline to nourish and wisely move the body. One doesn't climb a mountain or run a race without proper stretching and strengthening muscles and tendons. It's also wise to strategize the route, check the weather and "gear up" the mind to be ready for what's ahead. Preparing for the day with intention is a discipline and takes practice.

Preparation can be a well-known routine, but it's not a recipe and needs to be open to alterations as the practice matures. For example, when I was a gymnast, we never touched a single piece of equipment until everyone on the team gathered on the mats to stretch together for a good 20 minutes. We often got into pairs and helped stretch each other, pushing down on the other person's shoulders or back with a pressure one couldn't assert themselves. We'd check in along the way: "Any sticking points today?" "How's the pressure?" "Breathe!" The captains of the team led us through a known sequence of stretching from neck to pinky toes, parts of which I still use today.

Getting my body to awaken by gently stretching and moving into easy and then more rigorous exercise is what works for me. But as I said, this isn't a recipe for your success. My urging is to develop a routine that works for you. Once my body is fully inhabited, I like to move into a short meditation to settle my mind. Sometimes this is a very spiritual experience, feeling connected with something beyond myself. Sometimes it's just a few minutes of calm. Either way, the benefits of a mindfulness practice are well known.

Truth be told, I don't practice this routine every day. Some days I sleep in or lounge in bed daydreaming. Some days I must get up early to get to a meeting and it's all I can do to get dressed, shave and get in the car. In no way is the discussion of a "practice" a process of shaming myself or anyone else into doing something they don't want to do. But I can ask myself how the current practice, whether conscious or not, is preparing me for my day.

In my role as healer, what will serve me best? By the way, everyone has a healer within them. It's a natural part of being a human being. Think of a simple cut on your finger – the body is hard-wired to coagulate the blood and begin closing the wound. This is a physical internal healer. Outwardly, at our best, I think we are also hard-wired to be empathetic and helping toward others. Yes, this is a traditionally feminine attribute. But with the aggressiveness of a world in despair, don't we all have a role to play in bringing healing to bear, even if only in the domains in which we have impact, at home, at the office, or walking down the street of our local town?

As a healer, I need to bring my best self forth and for me, that means practicing some form of intentional, disciplined morning routine. One thing that's helped me think ahead regardless of how much time I've taken to get prepared is to share my intention for the day with my wife. Most days, we text each other with a quick affirmation and intention. That way we have something to look back on at the end of the day to see how it played out or how it served me.

Shakti Principles and finding balance

We've gotten where we are in the world from a very male dominated model of leadership. That's both wonderful and frightening. It's wonderful to look at the technological advances in healthcare, food production and military might. It's frightening because some of those advances have come at a huge cost to the environment and the welfare of a growing percentage of the world population. We've overlooked or forgotten the context of our relationships with sustainability and well-being. This might begin sounding like proselytizing or politicizing the point. When I feel this way, I'm learning to check my ego. Is it feeling threatened? Is it afraid of being phased out, unnecessary or marginalized? If that's the case, there is an opportunity to broaden the conversation. Learning more about a feminine model of leadership called "Shakti" has been inspiring and enlightening.

In their book "Shakti Leadership," Nilima Bhat and Raj Sisodia describe this feminine principle this way:

> *"Shakti is the abundant, unlimited fuel, the power of life that makes electrons move and galaxies grow and seeds sprout and trees flower. By learning to tap into that unlimited source, you can have power* ***with*** *others, rather than power* **over** *them... All over the world, societies, cultures, religions, philosophies, art forms, and literature make reference to and draw upon feminine energy personified in Mother Goddess. Much of physical existence is given a feminine identity, such as when we refer to Mother Nature or Mother Earth. Yet for virtually all of recorded history, the feminine has been controlled and subjugated by the masculine, which deep down secretly fears the Mother's unfathomable depth and creative power... To become balanced and integrated, organizations of all kinds need to value and cultivate feminine energies and qualities within their cultures – on the part of both men and women."*[4]

As I embrace these energies little by little, moment by moment, I find more available the potent resources of surrender, vulnerability, receptivity, flow, intuition, gentleness, and patience. In turn, I can focus without missing the forest for the trees, reason and strategize with less unintended impact and find confidence and strength without being overbearing or acting at the expense of others. I am more balanced when I gain strength after being open and discipline after being gentle.

I'm thrilled to see women's leadership forums, women's business groups, and women's rights being championed. But if

---

[4] Shakti Leadership by Nilima Bhat and Raj Sisodia, p. 5-6

only women are having these conversations, what happens to the men in power? There will not be an inclusive transition if they are left out and the result will be equally unsustainable. The men currently in power will not acquiesce without a violent fight and will not simply recede. I don't think we have the luxury of time to afford to the pendulum swinging too far the other way (*all* leaders being women) before finding a middle ground.

And so, it is vital to acknowledge the two parts of our energetic being: both masculine and feminine. Both are there, both are needed, and we desperately need to bring them into balance.

"Compassionate Response" is formed

I struggled with how to reconcile these two parts of me for much of my early career. When I was young, many people saw me as sweet, gentle, boyish, and puppy-like. It wasn't until I started playing football as a freshman in high school that I began building a stronger physical core. I quickly found gymnastics as well, ramping up the broadening of my shoulders and the confidence in myself. Following my dad's career path, I started working as a "runner" at the Chicago Board of Trade just after graduating from high school. I learned that I didn't quite fit into the locker room atmosphere but was intrigued enough to start an options trading business there a year out of college. I knew I had other work to do in the world that involved listening, collaboration and healing, but thought that could wait. I had to accomplish something first I thought! And so, 5 years became 10 and 10 became 15 and then 17.

Catalyzing a change was a traumatic exit from the business into a soul-searching curiosity about how to develop this other side of me – in fact how to reconcile both sides together. Something in me was stirring. Looking back, I think it was my inner healer being called to action. I started receiving calls to help people through difficult challenges with relationships, financial matters, and heath crises – literally calls for healing.

The only context I had for this at the time was the healing model I grew up with of being a Christian Science Practitioner – one who dedicates their life to offering prayerful support to seekers of spiritual truths based on the Bible and the teachings of a nineteenth century metaphysical pioneer named Mary Baker Eddy. Without going fully into the philosophy of what became a religion in the early 1900's, I will say there is a stunning simplicity and beauty in the core teachings of original wholeness and positive, peaceful thinking. Unfortunately, I witnessed the culture getting stuck in the early 1900's when the founder died and wasn't able to continue evolving critical thinking and current circumstances with advances in health care and awareness of impact on communities around them. Following a system or process that is unable to evolve with new information or adapt to differing circumstances becomes needlessly risky and naïve.

I saw the balance of the feminine qualities as healer as a possible career that may last the rest of my life. While I still consider myself a healer, the form of a religiously affiliated practitioner, lasted only for about 3½ years. But the seeds of my next career had been planted. My company, "Compassionate Response" was born as a vehicle to witness people's stories and challenge them to be their best self by recognizing and embracing innate potential. Still bringing love to bear on the human spirit, this form of healing operated in a business environment, where, I believe, there is the most leverageable force for good we have.

As a side note, I found many fellow travelers along this path at events supported by my local Conscious Capitalism chapter. The stated purpose of this organization is to "elevate humanity" through the practice of business as a force for good. Cultivating a new consciousness of how to lead and conduct business around a stakeholder-centric model required a radically different foundation of power – a feminine model that is systems rather than individually based.[5]

Somewhere along the way, a mentor suggested I would make a good mediator. I didn't really know what that meant other than he thought I had a calm demeanor. Following this comment, I took a few courses and found I was indeed a natural at accepting multiple perspectives on a topic, none of which held the whole truth or reality.

Part of the training involved building a strong "observer" in me that wasn't swayed or afraid of conflict. I learned how to listen to what was going on inside my head and manage it so I could listen with more empathy – and skepticism. I

---

[5] For more information, see www.consciouscapitalism.org

found the deepest compassion lay at the intersection of open kindness and wary skeptic. Certainly, kindness is part of accepting someone's story as simply their version of truth at any given moment. But growing the skeptic in me allowed a certain objectivity that didn't get inducted into their story. The fact that they believed their story was enough. I didn't have to believe it – I just got to listen to it and be able to understand the needs of the individual living it.

My feminine heart was opening, preparing itself for true, modern day warriorship – meeting in a place beyond my terms or theirs. I found deep resonance with Rumi's words *"Out beyond the ideas of right-doing and wrong-doing, there is a field. I'll meet you there. When the soul lies down in that grass the world is too full to talk about."*

One day early on in my new career, I struck up a conversation with a woman on a bus about conflict and how to hold it in a more graceful, effective way. It turns out the leadership team within her organization was struggling with internal conflict, and she asked how I'd deal with it. I jumped in, speaking from my heart about how resolution was less about fixing and more about learning to respond with compassion. Hearing and acknowledging each other had more impact than finding out who was right and who was wrong. As you might guess, I was hired by that organization and my new business, "Compassionate Response" was born.

As my talents and confidence grew, so did the business. Eventually I found myself working with individuals who knew they had more potential, knew there was more to life and knew they could be more effective leaders. They also appreciated simply being witnessed for who they were. I began receiving invitations to work with senior leaders and their leadership teams, guiding and coaching them to be in less conflict with themselves and others and finding a genuine path of conscious leadership. Eventually I started a roundtable of CEOs through Vistage Worldwide so they could help each other while I acted as their guide. With each step I found a new level of challenge to balance and blend my feminine healer and my masculine warrior.

This is my story of how I found the strength to build my practice by first opening my heart. I share it here as an example of why I believe the modern-day warrior and thought leader who is trying to offer guidance to a troubled world must begin with the heart.

Purification of Purpose

The final piece worth naming is about love itself. Love is not a word used in typical corporate circles. Love is, at its core a feminine energy although it can be experienced from and through all forms of energy. Love heals. Love embraces. Love is.

What does it feel like to be bathed in love? For me it's like being shepherded and purified. In this place I know something of who I am at my most elemental core, even if I can't articulate it. It is a reminder not to let someone else's expectations and judgments be imposed on me. It is a bodily acceptance of my basic goodness. Here, the purpose the Universe has for me and the purpose I feel I have for the world, blend. No separation between us. Co-creating how the day unfolds from the basis of Love (more on this in the next chapter). Being shepherded is to trust I'm in my right place, doing right work and being taken care of.

Growing up, the best reference I had of this sense of being shepherded was from the Bible, specifically the 23rd Psalm. Every time I read it, or it was read to me, I felt a kind of purifying balm. In her book, *Science and Health with Key to the Scriptures,* a text I grew up reading daily, author Mary Baker Eddy substitutes the word "LOVE" for "The Lord" in her interpretation of this Psalm. I always felt the presence of divine Love when I read this poem. I felt it wholly and purely. I was comforted and inspired. Below is this text. Read through it slowly to feel that same warm glow of a mother's love surrounding and bathing you.

> *[DIVINE LOVE] is my shepherd; I shall not want.*
>
> *[LOVE] maketh me to lie down in green pastures: [LOVE] leadeth me beside the still waters.*
>
> *[LOVE] restoreth my soul [spiritual sense]; [LOVE] leadeth me in the paths of righteousness for His name's sake.*
>
> *Yea, though I walk through the valley of the shadow of death, I will fear no evil: for [LOVE] is with me; [LOVE'S] rod and [LOVE's] staff they comfort me.*

> *[LOVE] prepareth a table before me in the presence of mine enemies; [LOVE] anointeth my head with oil; my cup runneth over.*
>
> *Surely goodness and mercy shall follow me all the days of my life; and I will dwell in the house [the consciousness] of [LOVE] forever.*[6]

In his book about the 23rd Psalm, sheep herder Phillip Keller shares his first-hand experience as a shepherd. He says, *"It is significant that to be at rest, there must be a definite sense of freedom from fear, tension, aggravation and hunger. The unique aspect of the picture is that it is only the sheepman himself who can provide release from these anxieties. It all depends upon the diligence of the owner whether or not his flock is free from disturbing influences."*[7] Imagine for a moment what the sense of freedom that we are taken care of fully and lovingly must feel like on a moment-by-moment basis. And if we are the sheep, who is the shepherd keeping us safe from disturbing influences?

To me this is the mother's love, the gentle yet all-powerful Love finding a receptive heart in us. My goal here is not to get overly scriptural or religious, even in the metaphor of being taken care of by our mother love. And yet when it is from here that I face the chaos and disruption of the world around me, I find a different opportunity. Rather than being overwhelmed with sadness and despair, I find strength and

---

[6] Science and Health with Key to the Scriptures, Mary Baker Eddy, p. 578:5-15

[7] A Shepherd Looks at Psalm 23, Phillip Keller, p. 36

grace to find islands of wisdom right in front of me. Here, guided and guarded by the power of Love, I connect with all others who are also trying to find sanity amidst ruined dreams, collapse, and an uncertain future.

At times, I'm tempted to stay within this little zone of comfort and perceived safety. But even that seems to be invaded by disruption and misunderstanding today. So, I'm moved to stay on the edge of my learning and bring a sense of love to the circles I move in. Over the last decade that has been in coaching conversations with senior leaders and entrepreneurs who lead business operations and companies. I do not expect to change the increasing complexity of the world around me through these conversations. I am simply moved to bring my wholehearted self to each conversation. When I stand firm on the ground of mother love, I am doing the best I can do with what I have. To be love. To be on solid ground. To be on home base.

Start with Heart

And so, the day begins. In the East, we awake into our vision and reaffirm our purpose. In the Southeast, the Owl of Compassion reminds us to immerse ourselves in unconditional love and forgiveness. In the South we feel into the heart space of the feminine divine. The energy of love bathes the day in healing. Everything is divinely orchestrated, and nothing is left out. Even before our thinking mind begins its analysis, we know, deeply and intuitively that all is well, and we are loved exquisitely. We're right where we need to be.

SOUTHWEST

Co-creating with the Universe

Quotes for the Southwest:

"The most important decision we make is whether we believe we live in a friendly or hostile universe." – Albert Einstein

"We are what we repeatedly do. Excellence, then, is not an act, but a habit." – Aristotle

It's the repetition of affirmations that leads to belief. And once that belief becomes a deep conviction, things begin to happen." – Muhammad Ali

"Be thankful for what you have; you'll end up having more. If you concentrate on what you don't have, you will never, ever have enough." – Oprah Winfrey

"There are only two ways to live your life, one is as though nothing is a miracle. The other is as though everything is a miracle." – Albert Einstein

"In difficult times carry something beautiful in your heart." – Blaise Pascal

PRACTICE:

Facing to the Southwest - *Co-creating with the Universe*

I am an integral part of something much bigger than "me."

The entire Universe is working with me – creating my path just as I am creating it.

I know that what I appreciate today will appreciate.

No matter the difficulty I carry beauty, gratitude, and confidence in my heart.

Surrender into the flow of Life.

Inspired Views

Facing this direction, I see one my favorite places in the world: the American Southwest. I love it for the playful dance of color and light; the high desert landscapes of orange and pink light glancing off sage brush and brilliant blue skies; the vast open spaces with Hispanic flair for warmth, color, and texture. It's no wonder that so many artists go to find inspiration in the deserts of the Southwest. Perhaps they come to feel the presence of a power outside themselves as I do when standing beneath the red rocks of Zion and Bryce Canyon National Parks. Is it the magnificent expanse of nature's beauty that acts as the artist's muse? The Southwest is the direction in which to look outward, to find faith and connection with all that is, and to pause long enough to find the depths of gratitude for everything around you.

The high desert is a place of contrasts. It can be both very hot and very cold, sometimes in the space of the same day. It is abundant in beauty and scarce in precipitation. To me it is a place of literal awe, and awe is a beautiful place to begin the journey of gratitude and serendipity. As the Warrior's Compass is about navigating from the comfort of a place of what's known to an often uncomfortable and unsettling place of unknown, a mechanism to calm anxiety is needed. The power of gratitude is a beautiful place to begin.

Finding gratitude

What does it take to feel grateful? For me it takes a pause. It's when I gently but resolutely and intentionally suspend the incessant inner skeptic and assume positive intent from the world around me. Once that voice is less insistent, a small space opens for noticing and then appreciating the tiniest things around me. Based on "what I appreciate, appreciates," I willingly begin a quick list of the many blessings I've been given.

There is incredible power in gratitude. In "The Five-Minute Journal," authors Alex Ikonn and UJ Ramdas write,

> *"Even after cutting through the smoke of Law of Attraction-style belief systems, gratitude has been shown to be quite transformative in humans ranging from students to retirees... A 2003 study by Emmons and McCullough found that keeping a daily gratitude journal leads to better sleep, reductions of physical pain, a greater sense of well-being, and a better ability to handle change."* [8]

When I was a child, my mother had a wonderful way of teaching me a lesson when I was annoyed, arguing with one of my siblings or complaining about something someone else did that I didn't like or agree with. She'd send me to my room with pen and paper and ask me to write ten things I

---

[8] Counting Blessings Versus Burdens: An Experimental Investigation of Gratitude and Subjective Well-Being in Daily Life, Emmons and McCullough 2003.

was grateful for – or if I was especially cranky, the list would grow to twenty-five. I wasn't to come out of my room until the list was complete.

You can imagine the consternation of a child expected to change attitudes quickly, especially when I felt justified in my anger and contempt. When I complained there was simply nothing to be grateful for about a situation, my mom would encourage me with a question like, "Did you like the color of the dress or blouse your sister was wearing?" I'd mutter something like, "oh I guess," and write down "#1: I'm grateful for the color red." I could slowly find a #2 and #3 and soon the list was complete. I typically forgot what I was angry or upset about. Now I may remember this activity with much more elegance than there was at the time. Since my mom passed away when I was 27, I couldn't corroborate the story other than with my siblings who all had their own version and recollection of the so-called "punishment." We all agree that making gratitude lists was effective and we still make them today, especially when things don't seem to be going well.

Gratitude simply is the feeling you get when you genuinely say, "Thank you." It's the feeling of joy that someone else has done a good deed and you've been impacted in a positive way, no matter how small or large. It's the smile you give to someone when they say hello or just help you bag your groceries or open the door for you. When intentional, it takes on an even more powerful, physical effect. *"One study found that people who simply thought about watching their favorite funny movie actually increased their endorphin levels (the chemical your brain produces to make you feel happiness and well-being) by 27 percent."*[9]

Have you ever experienced that wonderful feeling when something good happens on the heels of being grateful? I remember sitting at the kitchen table in my first house. As I recall, my wife and I were paying a few bills related to an issue with our plumbing and grumbling a bit about how we didn't deserve to deal with this problem – it must have been caused by the previous owners, we thought. By a stroke of chance, we decided to find something to be grateful for. We had fun thinking of all the things about the home we liked and found celebration in, including the plumber who had fixed the problem and the money we had to pay for it. We agreed we loved this home and decided we could easily stay here for many more years. Literally within days, we drove by a home a mile and half away we had never seen before and commented on how beautiful it was – in fact it felt like our dream home. It was for sale, so we called our realtor and asked about it. We decided to make an offer that day, it was accepted, and we put our house on the market and sold it within a few weeks. That was the home we gave birth to and raised our children in for the next 20+ years. We were blown away by the power of gratitude to bring such goodness into our experience.

---

[9] American Physiological Society April 3, 2006 – cited in The Five-Minute Gratitude Journal p. 263

Accepting the Skeptic

At this point, you might be thinking, "oh boy, this is some far side of woo-woo Law of Attraction stuff." Your skepticism is creeping back in, isn't it! Remember, this book lays out how I found a way to make sense in a world that seemed to be falling apart at an increasing rate. When in despair, many people fall back to their religious up-bringing and try prayer. So, while that skeptic might be asking to say a few words, maybe it's time to let it speak. What we keep squelched eventually comes out another way, often un-skillfully.

So, let it speak! My skeptic says something like, "okay, I get the power of gratitude, but mentioning the Universe is too close to be saying God for me and that stuff is all made up anyway." Okay, perhaps it is. And if there is collapse, disruption and wild storms brewing please DO batten down the hatches. And find a way to consider the path you've been on for your life to date. Think of the times you didn't know where to turn and, looking back, you found your way after all. How did that happen? Why did that happen?

The inner skeptic ultimately wants something for us, but it asks in a very childish, un-skillful way. When I've taken the time to listen to what it really wants for me, what it's really trying to discern, I get more patient and curious. Invariably, my patience invites more gentleness and openness from the skepticism. Pretty soon, I'm willing to listen with less judgment and opinion. Wherever your skeptic is right now, whatever it might be saying, take a moment to make friends with it. What does it really want for you anyway?

Co-creating Your Path

For most of my life, I've lived in the center of the United States, often called the Midwest or Great Lakes region. Because it's mostly flat, there aren't too many opportunities to see out from great vistas like a mountaintop. And, while we can certainly get lost anywhere, I find it easier to forge a new path in the woods if I know the general topography and trust I'll find my way back to my starting place if needed. When I really challenge myself, I try to have this same trust when hiking in the mountains and in unfamiliar territory.

When I walk through the woods, whether on a deer trail or just going cross-country to the next path, I often think about how I decide to put my foot down a little to the left or a little to the right. How do I decide? Am I following an intended path? Do I see something ahead that I want to see more closely? Am I forging the path, or is the path calling me? Ultimately, I always land on one answer: yes. The path is creating me as I am creating the path.

Think about that for a moment. Every footstep, every decision you make is a product of both your goals, intentions and knowledge, and something about the way that calls you forward – at the same time. That is a path co-created. When I surrender into this co-active process, I feel less scared, less responsible for making a mistake and more willing to move into what appears to be unknown.

I call the other side of this co-creation equation, "Universe," "Source" or "Great Spirit" in the native tradition. This path needs equal parts of imagination and faith because it relies on an intangible force. It is an energy which encompasses broadly many religious views of spiritual reality without getting tied to a certain dogma (at best, just different road maps to the same destination). This view is a choice – one that Einstein spoke of when he said, *"The most important decision we make is whether believe we live in a friendly or hostile universe."* If it is indeed friendly, I might as well learn how to cooperate with it. If it is hostile, then fear will likely drive every action and that is not a way of traveling I want to pursue. I trust with Victor Hugo, that *"all the forces in the world are not more powerful than an idea whose time has come,"* my grandfather's favorite and oft quoted saying.

I can't think of a better partner to help me navigate the craziness of the world around me. Especially since the noise is only getting louder. I am never lost. I am never alone. I have full capacity to move forward into the unknown, knowing my path is always being co-created.

Imagine arriving at the intersection of two streets – one called "Envision" and the other called "Cooperate" and something wonderful happens. Suddenly you're able to see just slightly around the corner. Things happen that seem beyond coincidence on a regular basis. It's a rather magical junction of being in flow. To "envision" is my job. My opportunity to take the time, even for a slight moment, to consider what's possible rather than see only roadblocks and malintent. To "cooperate" is what the Universe is doing at any given moment, and my opportunity to follow. Envisioning without cooperating is unfinished work, either a burdensome responsibility or a naïvely blind trust. Recognizing my role in creating what's ahead as well as the sense of surrender that may be required, gets me in the right mental space to feel gratitude.

The day on The Warrior's Compass began in the East with a powerful vision and purpose that dreamed us into existence. Here, we pick up on that vision and actively *en*-vision what might be ahead. This path requires some imagination of what things might look like in the future. It's a dreamlike sequence that doesn't appreciate the confines of consensus reality; in fact, the "that will never work" type thinking inhibits it. (That's just your new friend the inner skeptic just weighing in.) It's also a path of *co*-operation. This path requires some sense of humility and trust. It's not a path for everyone (but everyone is on it). It is my path and I'm proud of it. To travel this road is to appreciate what the voice of my inner skeptic has to offer and agree to travel with it as my friend rather than something which holds me back.

When just enough dreaming into 'what might be' is coupled with the right amount of trust that Source conspires with us, there is a place of confident anticipation from which I can enjoy this moment and keep reaching for the next. This is true even in a business context. For example, when a well-designed product is produced (supply) and meets the desires of the marketplace (demand), people are satisfied, and businesses sell products – everyone is happy. Efficient and effective economies are built on this platform of balance in supply and demand.

Consider what your life could look like if you gave yourself the gift of momentarily suspending, or even befriending skepticism, and dreamed into what you really want. You trust that when you put something on the wind, the Universe responds. Would you wake up each day with a different reason to get out of bed? While I never know just how far or near the propitious intersection of envisioning and cooperating is (and sometimes I get very lost along the way), the feeling of standing in the center of the intersection, smiling, knowing, happy and in awe, is always worth the effort to get there.

At the beginning of this book, I shared a Native American poem called "Lost" that begins with these words:

> *"Stand still. The trees ahead and the bushes beside you are not lost."*

This standing still for me is the remembering that I'm never just forging ahead by myself. I am in the presence of a sublime power far beyond me. And that power needs me to co-create with. So, I stand still, remember what I'm about, why I'm here, and then step boldly forth on my path. I am not lost.

Surrender

Without confronting the fear of surrendering, the Warrior cannot move forward. I've had to make peace with that statement daily. For most of my life, the word *surrender* implied weakness, giving up and lack of courage. But when navigating into the unknown, there is no other way to travel but by letting go and moving with the flow of what's trying to happen. Imagine stepping into the flow of a river and trying not to go along with it. That's the opposite of surrender and only serves to keep us stuck in the status quo.

In Paulo Coelho's book, *The Alchemist,* the wise king says to the boy,

> *"People need not fear the unknown if they are capable of achieving what they need and want. We are afraid of losing what we have whether it's life or possessions and property. But this fear evaporates when we understand that our life stories and the history of the world were written by the same hand."*

To let go of all the stories we make up about what loss might look like or feel like, or how it conflicts with our ego's desire to be safe, is to understand the Universe conspiring for us rather than against us. Indeed, our path and the future perspective about that path are written by the same hand.

Listening to our mind's stories, we may never step into that river because its swift current appears dangerous, cold, and uncertain. But following the flow of life we grow in our trust in the river itself. Its very job is to flow, so why would we not trust it? Of course, this trust isn't achieved all at once. Trust of life's flow is a series of experiments with letting go of our small self – only to find a much larger true self to have always had our best learning in mind.

Building a practice of gratitude and letting go is the most powerful tool to navigate the increasing complexity of our days. Do this work with all your heart, as if it was ordained by Great Spirit herself – because it is.

WEST

Dreaming into the Sunset

ELEMENT: ***Earth:*** Earth symbolizes stability, groundedness, sustenance, physical abundance, understanding, security, dependability, and wisdom. Earth is a receiving, feminine element often described as Mother Earth. It is also powerful, grounded, and solid, often categorized as masculine qualities.

Quotes for the West:

"Your most important work is ahead of you, never behind you." – Stephen Covey

"Life can only be understood backwards, but it must be lived forwards." – Søren Kierkegaard

"Train yourself to let go of everything you fear to lose." – Yoda

PRACTICE:

Facing to the West - *Dreaming up the Sunset*

Imagine the arc the sun will travel today, high overhead. Feel the rays of light blazing a trail of warmth from the bottom of the spine, up along each vertebra and up over the top of the head, lifting me up to be an inch taller. I stand on solid ground, claiming all that will be and how I want to feel at day's end.

What might the day teach me?

What do I have to teach others?

Notice – be keenly aware of the assumptions that try to take root here. I am open to all outcomes and notice when I'm overly attached to them.

I step into my brilliance. Fully embracing my potential, I know what is needed for today.

Picking up a handful of earth, as if at the end of the day, I blow it all away with a simple breath. Everything I plan for, strategize about, and envision is held so lightly that I can still be open and allow everything to unfold naturally. Like a beautifully created Mandala that is created for this moment and then released, I feel present, light, without baggage and free.

Context

As the Warrior's capacities are built through this compass, there comes a moment to take stock of where you are and how far you've come. A place of stepping into your brilliance, finding the opportunity to take in the lessons learned and potentially the lessons to be taught to others. Imagining today's sunset is that opportunity. The physical sun has just arisen on this day and already we're imagining it setting.

It's as if you could watch a very quick overview of the day through time-lapse photographs of each event, thought, color of the sky and feelings of accomplishment along the way. Suddenly you're at the end of the day in your mind's eye and you're reflecting on what it was like. Did you touch people's hearts today? Did your intentions come to fruition? What can you celebrate? What impact did you have? What lessons did you learn? All that in about 30 seconds.

Why do this? The reason stems from the idea of beginning with the end in mind – an idea championed by Stephen Covey in his "*Seven Habits of Highly Effective People.*" This idea is Habit #2. Are you right now the person you want to be? Are you the person needed to accomplish everything you've set out to do today? Take a moment to think about that and be honest with yourself *without sliding into blame and shame.* Covey claimed that this habit requires using your imagination – using your brilliance to see something you cannot yet see with your eyes. It's a muscle really – the ability to not only set a powerful vision as you did in the East, but to envision it coming to fruition.

Leaving Home for your Dreams – and Invoking the Inner Critic

In the South, getting firmly grounded on your home base was vital. Here, it is time to metaphorically leave home and set out into the unknown, and then acting "as if" you're already there. Of course, since you have a solid grounding on what home really means, you get to carry all the qualities of being grounded with you. Now you're able to set a new course honoring your dreams. This is a new muscle, often fraught with fear, self-doubt, and a noisy, over-active inner critic. If these voices are present at this moment, it's likely you're in the right place. Your brilliance is rarely given the opportunity to shine for fear of being considered arrogant.

Inciting the inner critic isn't a place most people go willingly. Being a Warrior isn't for the faint of heart! And it's time to get over yourself and take the risk to consider your brilliance. You at your best, your most authentic and able to do what you set out to do, stepping into an unknown day ahead.

There are many techniques to deal with your inner critic. I think Rick Carson's *"Taming Your Gremlin"* is one of the best ways to graphically give that voice an identity outside ourselves. He teaches a way of creating an entire persona for this critic so we can more easily see it as something outside ourselves, or at least one of many voices within us, not the only voice as it typically seems to be.

Using this method nearly 15 years ago, I came up with an inner persona, a character who was much like an Italian mobster, all dressed in black, smoking a big cigar and always wearing sunglasses. He speaks with a raspy voice and his name is Guido. (Nothing personal is meant to anyone with this name!) He drives a big black Cadillac and carries a dusty cloud along with him wherever he goes like the character in the Peanuts cartoon named Pig-Pen. He has a refrain that says some version of, "You're so arrogant… what a dirt bag you are (sometimes using much more colorful expletives)." Giving my inner critic this much detailed characterization and apparent autonomy has the effect of making it laughable. When I can laugh rather than buy into the fear he means to invoke, I can see it – the critic – much more for what it is: a suggestion to play it safe, play not to lose, and play small. After all, consider the risk of playing big! Failure, humiliation, mistakes, judgment. Who wants to knowingly flirt with those ugly monsters?

Spending more time with Guido, getting to know him and his wily ways, I've been able to understand more about what he really wants for me. I started by acknowledging that he did in fact want something for me, even though it was being done in a very ineffective and unskillful way. The more I probed and gently asked him questions (through journaling), the more he softened. Risking driving him into more subtle, devious ways, I got close enough to him to finally offer a job upgrade from Mobster Critic. I began to understand his desire for me to humbly consider and take responsibility for my impact on other people. I was stunned when this first became apparent. For most of my life, I had listened to this guy warning me not to become an imposter and criticizing my attempts at being bold and courageous. Now, with a gentler listening to what he really wanted, underneath the mob boss garb was a bigger boldness. Take responsibility for my impact? Wow – he really had my genuine attention with this.

Being intrigued, I took the next step and offered him the job of Impact Monitor, if he'd let go of being the Mobster Critic. Honestly, I'm not sure he's given up the critic role, but he's certainly less intimidating when he walks in the door chewing on his big stogie. He continues to grow into his new title, or perhaps more accurately, I continue to hold him to a higher standard. I accept less of the criticism when I'm alert, and more of it when I'm stressed. Over time, I've gotten better at noticing the difference between arrogance and responsibility for impact. Like most things, it's a work in progress.

What's really going on here beyond a fun game with my psyche? I'm not a therapist or trained as a psychiatrist, so I can only share my experience. What I found was that I had a more balanced sense of the stories I told myself. They didn't swamp me as much or trigger me for very long. Sure the self-doubt and criticism still show up, but they have less effect on my equilibrium. Never underestimate the power of self-awareness!

Making friends with your inner critic is vital amid the chaos and confusion caused by not knowing what's next. Rarely will we take big risks, consider failure an option and possibly make a fool out of ourselves if we're only listening to our inner critic. We certainly don't need more to deal with from the inside. We already have plenty of uncertainty going on all around us. So, get to know your most monstrous parts. Start a conversation with him or her through active voice dialogue and be oh-so willing to challenge the way things have always been.[10]

A Funny Story

I've written this book in various places like coffee shops, beaches, sitting on my couch and in airport lounges. While writing this portion about Guido, no surprise – he showed up. I was typing away in a coffee shop between meetings on a Sunday afternoon. I was dressed nicely with a smart blazer complete with pocket square, as I like to do when going out to be with clients, or in this case going to dinner with several highly esteemed colleagues. Looking up from my screen, I realized my computer was just about out of power and leaned back to plug my charger into a wall outlet. Suddenly the chair slipped out from underneath me making a loud screeching noise on the tile floor and I landed upside down, sprawled

[10] Active voice dialogue is a method of journaling both sides of a conversation, connecting with, learning about, and trying to integrate various parts of inner selves, as if writing parts in a play. It is active and playful, and a very powerful form of therapy. More on this in the Northeast.

out on the floor, my chair now three feet away upside down. Everything and everyone in the coffee shop stopped. I think even the music in the background paused while everyone looked at me and gasped, not knowing whether to laugh or ask if I needed help. Finally, the barista behind the counter squeaked out a timid, but smirking, "Are you ok?" I answered with an embarrassed "sure," looked around, and laughed while picking up my chair and sat back down to write, acting like nothing happened.

The irony wasn't lost on me. Here I was headed to be with people who speak in front of large audiences, to whom I look up – while writing as if I had something worth saying (said Guido). He pressed me, "you really don't have it all together and you are a farce!" Could I really stand up to Guido? Here he was, trying to get the last laugh, literally. "Who are you to be writing this stuff?" he asked with a smug snicker. He loomed large and I was listening.

Because I was acting like nothing happened and protecting my pride, my fear of being seen as irrelevant or a fraud took over. I think what would have been more helpful to me in that moment is to acknowledge Guido, to accept that I didn't have things all together and that was okay. Could I love myself just as I was, a man with a pocket square sprawled out on the floor – a human being who falls down occasionally? What if I could celebrate that humanity? But in that moment, all I could do was to sheepishly accept my humanity and keep writing. It was a good lesson, and even represented a small step of progress in making friends with Guido.

This Day at its End

Facing the West is an act of courage and imagination. It is an opportunity to move from something known in the moment into a total unknown day ahead. It may have a plan, a purpose, and an intention, but I really have no idea if the car in front of me will slam on its brakes, causing me to crash into them or if I will win the lottery. And so, this is the time to dream into how I want the day to feel when I look at the sunset.

This day, at its end will be amazing; or it will be boring; or I'll forget to even reflect on what kind of day it was. Being intentional about my life has been all over the map. Others may think I'm super conscious of what I want and why I do things. But really, I have the same doubts and sound-asleep moments as everyone else. What's being named here is super aspirational and it's important to keep this mind. Even though Guido may chime in from his old role and make fun of what I'm attempting today, I still have the choice to listen or not. To be intentional or not. To love or not.

At the end of this day, I want to be exhausted, in a good way. The kind of exhaustion you feel when you've helped a friend carry a heavy suitcase up the stairs or had five client coaching sessions back-to-back. I feel well-used. My skills all came into service and shined brightly. I saw people for their potential and helped maximize it. At the end of this day, I don't want to feel like there's more I could have accomplished. I want my energy and my capacity to be so in sync that I can fall into a deep sleep with gratitude and satisfaction.

Take some time to picture what that would feel like for you. Without giving into to self-criticism, how do you want to feel at the end of your day? What would make today great? What qualities will be most needed and how did you embrace them? Come up with questions you can ask yourself at the end of the day. Here are a few I came up with many years ago. No, I don't ask them every day, either at the beginning or at the end. But somehow having them out there inspires me to give it my all.

Provocative Questions to Ask at the End of the Day:

- How did I dance at the edge of my comfort zone?
- How did I listen exquisitely?
- How did I live my purpose?
- How did I live as a whole-hearted, spiritual warrior?
- How did I expand the range of creative possibility in others and myself?
- How did I act as a good steward to my financial and ecological resources?
- How did I embrace paradox and hold it lightly?
- How did I grow healthy thoughts in my mind's garden?
- How did I build "right relationships?"

Open to Outcomes

Being open to outcomes while not being attached to those outcomes is no easy task. But it is a serious goal if you're aiming to play a bigger game in your life. What does it mean to be open to outcomes? First, it means that I do have certain outcomes I'm aiming for like being of service to others, taking care of myself physically, emotionally, and spiritually, loving unconditionally and getting paid well for the work I do. I have an intended outcome with my family to listen well, make sure they feel loved and to be in touch with them frequently. I have an intended outcome of staying married, having happy kids, and surviving their teenage years. I have an intended outcome to use my skills fully and to not get too lost or too frustrated while navigating through traffic and finding creative ways around it.

Second, being open means not being so attached to those outcomes that I miss the opportunity to learn something new, to be surprised or to slow down enough to appreciate an amazing maple tree in full autumn regalia. When I get attached to my outcomes, not only do I miss the spirit of them, but I miss sacred moments of seeing beauty right in front of me.

Let me give an example. As my kids were growing up, I started saving money for their college education. It seemed prudent to begin a savings account for them within months of their birth. I did well, contributing to their accounts every year. Partway down this practical track to saving for college, a unique opportunity came up for them to travel abroad for their junior year of high school. Paying the tuition for this program wasn't in my education budget and would throw off my plan! So, I tried to apply for scholarship money and financial aid, only to get turned down because of certain assets I owned.

At that point, I could have just said no, it wasn't in the cards for them to take advantage of this opportunity, because that money was earmarked for college. I was clearly attached to a certain investment outcome. In a way, this was playing small, only seeing one way for things to work out. Remember the concept in the Southwest, *"what you appreciate, appreciates?"* This was a perfect opportunity to appreciate all forms of education and co-create the outcomes with the Universe! I did end up paying for both my kids to take part in an exceptional opportunity to study in Beijing for their junior year of high school and used some of their college funds to do so. What I didn't know was that my son would get a very generous merit-based scholarship to attend his university two years later. It all worked out, but on a very different timing than I could see at the time.

Noticing Assumptions

Part of the gift of not being attached to outcomes is noticing the assumptions baked into the outcomes. In my story above, I assumed that the amount I'd pay for college tuition was a set amount. I assumed "education" meant college education. I assumed that since I wasn't earning much money at that time, available funds would be limited and depleting. Instead, the experience was liberating and taught them how to be more global citizens. Had I noticed and been able to name the assumptions earlier, I may have been more open to other ways of looking at the bigger picture and found even more opportunities.

From this standpoint in the day – before it's even started, how do you question the assumptions that might color the outcomes you've intended? Well, first, it's important just to ask the question, "What assumptions am I making about this outcome, or about how this day will unfold?" That is a bold question and one that has no right answer. But it does deserve an answer.

We are hard-wired to make assumptions. It's our brain's way of conserving energy so every decision doesn't have to go through a full if/then scenario. That makes sense, right? So why interrupt the way our brain has evolved? Because habits are hard to break. Once we're on a track, we assume we'll always be on that track. Stepping just a bit to the right or left is easier if we're not in a big rut. And, so the best way to stay out of big ruts is not to get into small ones.

I loved playing with this theory when I was commuting to downtown Chicago every day on the train. I challenged myself to take different trains in the morning and to sit in different seats (often to the chagrin of people who liked their regular seat). When I got off the train, I had a 15-minute walk to my office. I challenged myself to take a different route every day. Instead of blankly walking the same route, I looked for new underground tunnels and new shops. Different seasons brought new challenges to stay indoors or outside as much as possible. After commuting this way for 17 years, I never missed a train and always enjoyed the new sights.

Of course, we'll never stop making assumptions. It's how we stay safe. But naming or even questioning the assumptions is healthy for achieving the outcomes you intend – and staying open to new outcomes along the way. It's also healthy for relationships and boundaries. Too often, boundaries are assumed, and are therefore fuzzy. The best leaders are clear about their boundaries and can name the assumptions they are making. Give it a try today. Start a conversation with someone about the assumptions you're operating under. It can be vulnerable territory, but well worth traversing.

The Teacher Awaits

There is a wonderful inner teacher awaiting you. She sits in the West, amidst adventure, purpose, and possibility. Take a moment to get to know her by facing the still dark sky with the morning sun at your back. Commune with her by dreaming into what the day has to offer ahead. Your inner teacher will respond with all kinds of opportunities for learning, finding humility and a more authentic response to possibility. Lean into all of it! Then with a sense of humor and detachment, rest all the possibilities in the palm of your hand and gently blow them into the wind.

Lessons from a Tibetan Sand Mandala

Many years ago, I traveled to New Zealand. Of the many incredible sights and experiences, one of the most enduring images I recall vividly was watching Tibetan Monks painstakingly create a sand mandala. I had never seen art more beautifully and lovingly created. Simple men, saffron and maroon-robed with the most tender smiling eyes I'd ever seen, laid down colored sand at a pace that ignored common sense, clocks and every-day measurement. Sometimes it looked like only one grain at a time was being placed with such exquisite attention to detail, I barely saw any progression. And yet, I could see that it was deeply meditative, and the brilliant circle of colors was indeed expanding.

The word mandala is a Sanskrit word for circle, representing the universe. According to Buddhist teachings, mandalas constructed from sand transmit positive energies to the surrounding environment, including to the witnesses who view them. They are believed to create a healing and purifying effect. Simply observing the creation of this mandala had a profoundly calming effect on me and I was compelled to watch for a long time.

The monks who weren't creating the mandala were more than happy to answer questions about what we were witnessing. They had been working on this mandala eight to ten hours a day for several weeks and were nearly finished. The symbolism of the design, I learned, was a floor plan of the sacred mansion that is life. It was truly a sight to behold and stirred me deeply.

But it was outside, under a covered awning and I wondered what would happen when the weather changed. How long would it be there for the townspeople to appreciate? I learned that when the piece of art was finished, it would be swept up into urns and later dispersed into flowing water. In this way, the healing and purification could flow out to the rest of the world. Symbolically, this fantastic, geometric creation these talented men had worked so hard on, prayed over, and then destroyed, sent out the message that things which are visible are insubstantial.

I was overwhelmed, disturbed, and saddened by this practice. Clearly, I had something to learn about impermanence, meditation, and joy. It's taken me many years to come to terms with my sadness about seeing beauty, scattered away in an instant. I love objects that are well-designed, and I'm rather attached to my sleek sports car, thank you very much. Meditating on impermanence seemed fruitless at first, probably because I was so focused for most of my life on accumulating, growing, and succeeding. Here was a life-lesson just waiting for me to stop by. Here I am so many years later, deeply grateful I was challenged to see beauty differently. It is with the spirit of the Tibetan monks I offer the opportunity to take a handful of earth, symbolizing all my hopes and dreams for the day – and blow them into the wind. Now open, without baggage, I am light and free.

NORTHWEST

Permission to Fail

Quotes for the Northwest:

"If we are not able to let go of what we know, there is no room for a larger wisdom to come in." – Karen Kimsey-House

"I hope that in this year to come, you make mistakes. Because if you're making mistakes, then you're making new things, trying new things, learning, living, pushing yourself, changing yourself, changing your world. You're doing things you've never done before, and more importantly, you're doing something."– Neil Gaiman

"Every adversity, every failure, every heartache carries with it the seed of an equal or greater benefit." – Napoleon Hill

"You'll always miss 100% of the shots you don't take." – Wayne Gretzky

"I have not failed. I've just found 10,000 ways that won't work." – Thomas Edison

"Success is not built on success. It's built on failure. It's built on frustration. Sometimes it's built on catastrophe." – Sumner Redstone

"It's not what happens to you, but how you react." – Epictetus

PRACTICE:

Facing toward the Northwest - *Permission to Fail*

I give myself full permission to suck, to mess up and make mistakes today, and all the previous days I've walked this earth.

I accept all parts of myself as necessary to be whole – light, dark, messy, brilliant and say a playful "ta daaa" when I fall into the inevitable muddy puddles. I thank them.

I embrace creativity, playfulness, and resilience today. I love you. I'm sorry. Please forgive me. Thank you.

Unconditional love and permission to fail

When I flushed the owls in Nebraska during the summer of 2008 during a solo walk around my property in the Sandhills, I didn't know the extent of how they would teach me lesson upon lesson over the next decades. As I told my life story around the fire for several days, three themes became very clear. The first one, as I named in the Southeast was one of unconditional love shown to me so gracefully by my mother and embraced as a quality I knew would make me a better person. But it was this second theme of failure, mistakes and regrets represented by the second owl, that most challenged me.

In the Western world, failure is considered a dirty word. We don't typically like to fail, much less own our failures. Until this owl showed up in my life, I was no different. I considered my poor decisions and mistakes as something to be ashamed of and hoped nobody would find out that I hadn't lived up to my best and highest potential. After all, I had a reputation to keep up. You see, I was kind of the "Golden Boy" growing up who rarely had to own up to his mistakes, rarely got caught doing anything wrong and even got the "snips and snails, and puppy dog tails" award one year at my summer camp because the counselors saw me as such a good little boy who only had good, innocent thoughts.

Hiding our failures

While I certainly had one in me who wanted to be a good little boy and often was, I also did things that were mischievous, uncaring, and sometimes downright harmful. Now, you might hear me being hard on myself here. Of course, everyone makes mistakes and does things they're not proud of along the course of their life. Whether it was treating my siblings poorly, joining my friends in calling other kids names or stealing a pack of gum from the grocery store, I wasn't proud of being that kid. I hid the actions from everyone, including myself. What other people saw later in my life was either great confidence and calm, or an arrogant, self-righteous, better-than exterior. Hiding didn't do me any favors when it became a way of protecting myself from really being seen. The exterior hardened into a kind of armor that insulated but also exacerbated the distance between the hidden and the seen.

This was intensified by being raised in a religion that focused on spiritual truths over material untruths and ugliness. It was like a spiritual bypass around things that should have been dealt with head-on rather than swept under the rug. Of course, I had my share of humiliating moments like taking the gum that I stole back to the store and apologizing and going to my neighbor's house to tell them I was sorry for getting in trouble with their child. But I don't know that those lessons really sunk in that sometimes, yes, we're just naughty.

I remember one time when a friend and I were riding our bikes around the neighborhood and a police car drove by, making his rounds. Granted, this was a very safe, mostly white, suburban neighborhood and the officer was very friendly. But it was the early 70's and my friends all had older siblings who were involved in anti-Vietnam war protests years earlier and had a general dislike of authority. I must have unconsciously picked up on their sentiments and as the police car drove by, I stuck my thumbs in my ears, waved my hands, and stuck out my tongue, saying "Pig!" to the policeman. I was probably 9 years old at the time, and I panicked at being seen as a naughty kid by the authorities. When the squad car stopped and backed up, I froze, knowing he had seen me and was about to teach me a life lesson.

As he came up to us, the police officer asked me to show him the face I had just done behind his back. Beet-red and deeply embarrassed, I showed off a timid "nah, nah, nah" face just as my parents were walking by with our dog. Ugh – if only I could take that moment back! Fortunately, the police officer was a kind man and probably knew he could make a difference in my life. I vaguely recall a conversation about respect, apologies and being our best self and ever since, I've had a deep respect for men and women in uniform, who at their best, serve a very difficult role in society. In the tumult of deteriorating race relationships in 2020, I remember this episode even more poignantly for how I was treated with respect even when I was not acting out of respect. That's a high bar for anyone to maintain.

But I shoved down that and so many other experiences and never talked about them with anyone. I was just too embarrassed to own that I had done anything disrespectful, unthinking, and unkind. When my parents asked what happened, I shrugged it off and didn't tell them the truth. There were other things even more egregious I did as I entered my teens that I also squashed down, armored up, and created a kind of shame story around. Some pieces of this shame are still with me, and I get embarrassed to think I did things that weren't right or were unkind. When that happens, this owl from the northwest swoops in to remind me to acknowledge my humanity and forgive myself. Embarrassment is normal but after a while it doesn't serve me only to be embarrassed.

When I give myself permission to fail, to be human and to have done things I'm not proud of, I can begin to find a gentle forgiveness and be aware of ways to make amends if needed. Otherwise, it's time to move on. Permission allows for the release of embarrassment and shame. It is a recognition that wholeness necessarily includes shadows.

This was especially cathartic back on my Nebraska land, telling my story in front of the fire. I started to see my not-so-good self as part of my whole self, a shadow side that had never been allowed to really be seen. While there were many things I wasn't proud of and never really owned up to, I was able to face the shame, embarrassment and regret about them squarely and honestly. "Could I really own those parts of myself?" "Could I love them?" I wondered out loud to the rising smoke into the night sky. Just as quickly as those words left my mouth came a ringing answer of unconditional love from another part of me… "Yes, they are an integral part of you and it's what makes you whole."

It's taken me several years to honestly understand that response and to accept my wholeness as naturally and fundamentally including darkness, shadow, shame, and ugliness. As I've accepted this, I've learned to courageously invite it into the light, ever so gently. Along the way, I've had the help of classes, retreats, counselors and an amazingly loving and accepting life partner who is so incredibly gentle I sometimes feel I don't deserve such kindness. Now I can more easily say, "Welcome shy one… it's okay to be here, to be scared and embarrassed and to want to make amends." "I'm just going to sit here beside you for a while."

This lesson is what the second Owl's playfully invites. I've learned to call it, "Permission to Fail." For it's in the permission I give myself that I begin to accept failure as part of my journey. When I can celebrate it as a necessary part of myself, I learn how to forgive myself and be ever so much gentler with myself. With permission also comes a shy welcoming. Not to taunt failure by jumping off cliffs and saying things without forethought, but with a simple invitation to be here, now.

A few years after finding this way of forgiving and being gentler, my colleague Adam Shames introduced me to his concept of "PTS" – or "Permission To Suck" – in a workshop he was leading. Adam is a master facilitator and founder of the Kreativity Network. It was his urging of his groups to accept this "PTS" mindset that got them out of their comfort zones just far enough to have fun playing musical instruments they'd never otherwise touch and explore innovative ideas they wouldn't normally consider. I thank Adam for the encouragement to continue evolving my take on this needed way of being and inviting the messiness of life.

Necessity of Failure

Now, giving yourself permission to fail is not an excuse for doing nothing and not addressing or not changing! That would just be way too convenient and yet another way to play small in the world. Sometimes it's a fine line, but it's one worth exploring, for just on the other side of the permission is a welcoming of a new way of doing things.

Permission to fail, and even failure itself is an opportunity for deeper introspection. Making mistakes often causes us to find a new or better way of doing things. So really, if you want to be successful, fail more often! IBM's former chairman and CEO Thomas J. Watson said,

> *"You are thinking of failure as the enemy of success. But it isn't at all. You can be discouraged by failure, or you can learn from it. So go ahead and make mistakes. Make all you can. Because remember, that's where you will find success."*

There is a wonderful Calvin and Hobbes cartoon by Bill Watterson, that shows Calvin casually walking along and suddenly finds himself face down in a mud puddle. Hobbes seems to watch with some trepidation as to what will happen next but has a sly smirk on his face. In the next scene, Calvin jumps up, mud all over his face, shirt, and pants, and says, "ta daaa!" That's the kind of permission to fail that gets me up in the morning. It inspires me to lighten up, not hold my reputation or my (perceived) dignity too tightly and offer my most messy moments a mud-faced, "ta daaa!"

Mindset of Fearlessness

I often reflect on what this mindset offers to the complexity, chaos, and conflict. If we don't have to get it right the first time, can have some light-hearted gentleness with ourselves and those around us, I wonder if we'd give each other a bit more latitude? And why is this a crucial element of warriorship?

Remember, a warrior traditionally is one who willingly puts themselves at the margins of a community or tribe to protect others. One who willingly risks dying to remain committed to purpose and to follow a deeper inner calling and knowing. Where is the fear of failure in that kind of commitment? Would failure be dying in service? Or living despite the service? While I haven't had to face those kinds of life and death circumstances, I am learning to know what it means to live without fear of failure, and it has made all the difference in my life. As our world continues to struggle with climate collapse, racial inequities, and polarizing politics we can be emboldened by a full permission to fail quickly at trying new things, without shame. Maybe with this clearance we can begin finding more answers than questions. And if not, we'll certainly be able live with less stress about it.

Building a Practice – Or "Remembering"

This might sound much easier said than done, as most things are in life. It takes regular practice to face fear, chaos, and uncertainty gracefully – or even full of mud and mess. One practice that serves me well, especially in a pinch, is simply breathing with intention. There are many, many variations of breathing practices to explore, but one endorsed by the US Navy SEALs that brings quick physical calm and mental focus, is called box breathing. It's a technique that "helps you take control of your automatic breathing patterns to train your breath for optimal health and performance," says Mark Divine, former US Navy SEALs Commander and author of *The Way of the SEAL*. I've noticed when I feel most stressed, embarrassed, or uncertain about what to do next, this process reduces my blood pressure, and my heart rate drops.

The hardest part of this practice is remembering to do it when under pressure. I suspect during Navy SEAL training it becomes part of the regimen for soldiers about to enter a dangerous situation with uncertain outcomes. But given that most of us aren't Navy SEALs it's important to build a practice before it's needed even if the outcomes we face aren't life or death situations.

Remembering is the act of putting ourselves back together – literally re-membering. So, it fits that part of recognizing our wholeness begins with breathing, where our lives began as newborn infants. Once we are re-membered, the process of calm has already begun.

Next, simply notice as you breathe in with intention that your in-breath is climbing the left side of a box, to the count of 4. When you get to the top of the box, hold your breath easily at the top, to the count of 4. Then let it out slowly as you descend the right side of the box, also to the count of 4. At the bottom, as you move left to your original starting place, hold your out-breath at the bottom to the count of 4. Repeat this process 4 times in a row. And if you don't remember any of this, just breathe with intention, holding your breath at the top and bottom of each in and out breath. It's that simple – and that difficult.

Any practice of getting grounded and present will do when facing uncertainty. When we reconnect with our most essential self – that part of us which is distinct from the fear, shame, or stress of the moment, we are more able to discern how to act next. That action proceeds independent, or at least less dependent on the lifelong stories of who we think we are. This is our "unstoried" self.

The Key Ingredient is Gentleness

It is our unstoried self that gives us permission to fail, to not live up to our potential and to get stuck in our muddy stories. With that permission comes the very ingredient that allows us to open to what's wanting to emerge: *gentleness*. At various points on this compass so far, gentleness has been a key feature. In the Southeast, unconditional love requires a gentle warmth toward ourself and others. In the South, we reclaim our feminine healer, rooted in gentleness, nurturing and grace. Here, that gentleness gets turned inward to our most precious self. It is from here we can stand up after falling in the mud puddle and say "ta daaa" with a sense of humor and kindness. In some ways, it's a kind of magical letting go that happens. Without this letting go, we cannot claim true warriorship, which is why true north, the next direction, is where the warrior finally appears.

Magic Toothpaste

Several years ago, I was skiing with my wife (then girlfriend) in Colorado. It was our first run of the day, toward the beginning of our week-long vacation and I was eager to hit the slopes. One of the things I love most about my wife is her willingness to jump into something new even if it seems foreign. Being a life-long athlete and very adept at trusting her body, she agreed to try a brand-new sport in her 40's. We started slowly – to my many years as a skier perspective – and quickly to her new skier perspective. Part way down the run, she stopped and wasn't sure how to proceed, or if this was even something she wanted to do this day. In my ignorance and male "just do it" attitude, I didn't comprehend what she was experiencing and likely made her feel embarrassed for stopping. She became frozen with uncertainty and lack of the confidence she was feeling just an hour before.

We agreed to stop skiing for the day and quite quickly, my emotions started to pack my throat and brain with anger, resentment, and confusion. We had a very quiet car ride back down the mountain to our inn, but my passive aggressive blood pressure seeped out in drips and drags. Of course, she felt all my non-verbal disappointment with how the day was starting out and wasn't sure if she should defend herself or say, "I'm sorry."

Getting back to the room, still quietly resentful and confused, I changed my clothes and decided to brush my teeth. Looking at myself in the bathroom mirror as I put the toothpaste on my toothbrush, a thought, out of nowhere, flashed above my reflection as if in a visual thought cloud above my head: "what would it be like to skip over all my disappointment, the potential arguments of self-righteousness and wasted time, and get to the other side?" Of course, I didn't know what was on the other side, but it seemed a lot better than the current predicament. I finished brushing my teeth and considered what the day might look like at the end of it if I was able to let go – just patiently and gently let go of what seemed so important to me.

I left the bathroom and said something like, "let's start this day over again… what do you want to do?" Once she got over her shock that I wasn't getting grumpy and distant (what I too often do when I'm wrestling with something), we discussed walking around town, exploring some new areas and possibly even stopping by that open house around the corner as if we were interested buyers. It turns out we had an amazing day together and better yet, found a new layer of possibility in our relationship. We laughed about what might have been in that toothpaste to cause such a turn-around in my attitude in such a short amount of time. Hence, the "magic toothpaste" because there is a kind of magic to just letting something go.

In retrospect, I think this was a great example of what happens when we combine full permission to mess up with a big ole dollop of gentleness. We're able to nimbly change directions, consider other perspectives, lean into what's possible and be so much happier. Like so many things before, this is much easier to write about than it is to remember to do it. But it does get easier with practice, I promise.

Part of what happens when we give ourselves permission is a form of self-forgiveness for messing up in the first place. Ultimately, forgiveness to me is the giving up of the right to be right. Forgiving ourselves then is the giving up of being hard on ourselves for not being our best. It's good to be our best of course, but we're not always there. When I can give up being my best self all the time, everything just gets so much lighter. And not-surprisingly, I'm gentler with myself.

Forgiveness and Taking Full Responsibility

I learned of a Hawaiian forgiveness practice called *Ho'oponopono* many years ago. This word comes from *ho'o* (to make), and *pono* (right, or doubly right when repeated twice). It's an ancient practice for South Pacific islanders and there is a more "New Age" practice taught by healer Morrnah Nalamaku Simeona who was designated a living treasure of Hawaii in 1983. This simple 10-second practice releases the negativity held inside us and has a positive outward ripple effect. In that way, what we feel or think impacts those around us.

What always stood out to me about this practice was the resulting impact on others when I take full responsibility for working on myself. To me, taking full responsibility meant being conscious of what I think and do. Whatever happened to others after that was out of my hands. But the stories of this conscious ritual of reconciliation and forgiveness kept chasing me after getting divorced. Figuring out how to take full responsibility – my 100% responsibility, not anyone else's – seemed the only way I could move on with my life. When I finally opened the places that hurt and took responsibility for them, I found a wonderful sense of healing release. I also believe the work I was doing had ripples far and wide, the extent of which I don't even know.

Dr. Ihaleakala Hew Len, a Hawaiian therapist and healer explains: "*total responsibility for your life means that everything in your life – simply because it is in your life – is your responsibility.*" In other words, the distance between other people and me begins to disappear when I see my responsibility for how I perceive them and act accordingly.

Ho'oponopono is deeply personal work in four short phrases. The suggestion is to respond when a place for healing presents itself in your life by opening the place where hurt resides within you. Then, with deep humility, honesty, and courage, say these statements to yourself as many times as needed:

I love you.

I'm sorry.

Please forgive me.

Thank you.

These words and the sincere desire to mean them helped me heal from the effects of getting divorced. It helped me heal a long-standing separation from my family of origin. It has helped me heal from many small wounds suffered during arguments and remembrances of past injuries, both inflicted by me and on me. The words are part of the mystical ingredients in magic toothpaste. They continue to stretch me to give myself full permission to mess up. And to take full responsibility – my 100% when I do. They ripple outward on a wave of love, finding home in everything around us. Once on their journey, I can let go of an expected outcome, stand firm in my messy, muddy wholeness and with a courageous giggling, shout, "ta daaa!"

Perhaps it is in how we define "failure" that we begin to see the embedded opportunity. Perhaps the shame of doing things we're not proud of is part of what needs to be redefined.

Permission to fail, to have a dark side and to make mistakes, while not a blanket clearance to continue thoughtless, unkind behavior, is required of today's Warrior. The Owl of the Northwest shares its wisdom through gentleness, forgiveness, and patience. Too often, I ignore the subtlety of that gentleness and continue thinking of myself as small, insignificant, and wrong for my mistakes. And how this holds me back from my most important, my Warrior's work! I have daily opportunities for listening to this most misunderstood and overlooked owl. But I do so at my own peril. Arrogance steps in where humility is due. Bravado feels so much better than shame. Hiding feels so much safer than bringing light to the darkness. Still, the real work of the Warrior – the next chapter's main theme – waits and waits until we listen deeply to this owl's gentle message.

NORTH

The Warrior Emerges

ELEMENT: ***Air:*** Air is associated with the breath of life. It symbolizes intelligence, perception, learning, imagination, creativity. It has a natural upward movement, has a masculine archetype, and is often associated with the Sky Father, or Father Sky.

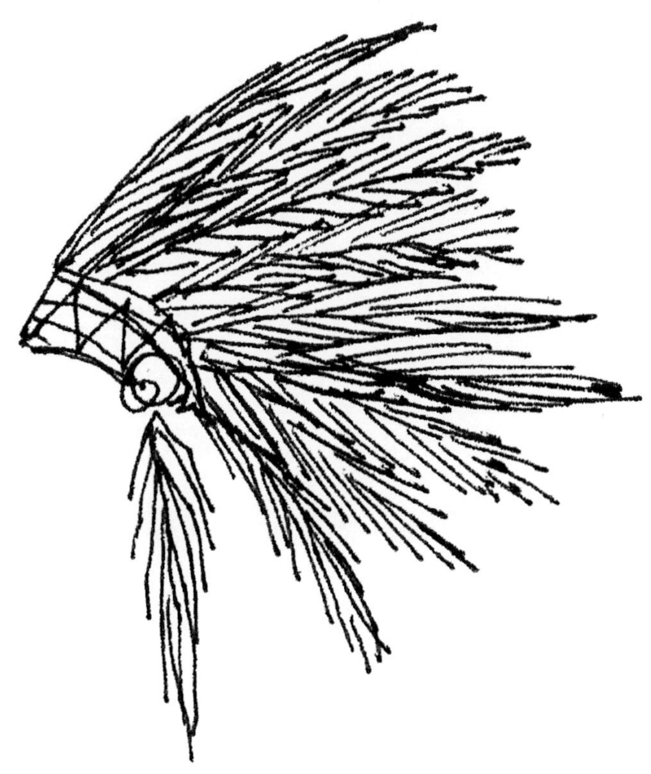

Quotes for the North:

"Out of every one-hundred men, ten shouldn't even be there, eighty are just targets, nine are the real fighters, and we are lucky to have them, for they make the battle. Ah, but the one, one is a Warrior, and he will bring the others back." – Heraclitus

"Fate whispers to the Warrior, 'You cannot withstand the storm' and the Warrior whispers back, 'I am the storm.'" – Unknown

"Inside everyone is a frontier waiting to be discovered." – Dances with Wolves

"Two roads diverged in a wood, and I – I took the one less traveled by, And that has made all the difference." – Robert Frost

"While despair might permeate the greater part of the nation, others achieved a new realization of the fact that only readiness for self-sacrifice could enable a community to survive. Some of the greatest saints in history lived in times of national decadence, raising the banner of duty and service against the flood of depravity and despair." – Sir John Glubb

"The Warriors arise when the people need protection. We step into this role of contribution and service, learning to assess what is possible and what is not. We are broken-hearted in witnessing what is being lost. We are exhausted from efforts that can no longer bear fruit. Yet we have abiding faith in the human spirit, in the capacity of people to be generous, creative, kind, and compassionate – no matter what. It is our faith in the human spirit that inspires us to undertake the discipline of training to be of service for this time." – Meg Wheatley

PRACTICE:

Facing toward the North - *The Warrior fully Emerges*

The full extent of the brave, courageous and deeply compassionate masculine arises in me with a whoosh of frozen air.

Today's accomplishments are infused with resilience, honor, and dignity.

My back is strong and straight. I feel the wind pushing and pulling me about, but like Willow wedded to Oak I am grounded by my deep roots and can sway with the wind effortlessly.

I choose to show up fully present and give my best to every endeavor. I also choose to let my belly be soft, open, and vulnerable. Courage meets compassion in a graceful balance.

I am life itself.

Catharsis

This book was written over many years. Every time I thought it was ready to be complete, some part of my life would offer a new lesson and a new way of putting my Warriorship into practice and I couldn't get past the previous (Northwest) chapter – the acceptance of a wholeness that includes darkness, not-knowing, and mistakes. Finally, toward the end of 2020 amid an ongoing pandemic and working from home for most of the prior 8 months I had a cathartic realization.

The insight was this:

> *Until I really learned how to practice gentleness to myself, not just give it lip service, but wholeheartedly embrace the Universe as unconditionally gentle, and fully give myself permission to embrace my wholeness with all its messiness, I could not claim my Warriorship.*

I couldn't write this chapter until I found a much deeper empathy for the wholeness of my fellow human journeyers – both those I appreciated and those I couldn't comprehend. That happened as I noticed the world crying out for gentleness amid waves of violence, illness, and polarization. There was a moment of deep emotional connection with everyone's suffering, past and present which could only be healed through gentleness. This sense of empathy disrupted the way I thought of and practiced empathy. No longer could it be available only for those I felt something for. With this discernment finally came a new ease of writing the keystone chapter of this book about the full emergence of Warriorship.

The Warrior Rises

At last, the Warrior – the one whom this book is from, to, and about, takes its full shape. But here's the key to the entire compass: *this* Warrior emerges from the soil of all the work done up to this point: each chapter has been a vital portion of a brave evolution. The mistake we make when thinking about the Warrior is believing he is only courageous and masculine, only required to train to physically fighting battles.

The battlefield of today is so increasingly complex and uniquely demanding that diligence, bravery, and ferocity – the Warrior's well-known fighting skills – need to be taken to a deeper level. In current times the Warrior who can "*bring the others back*" must necessarily be willing to be lost, disoriented and devastatingly, haltingly saddened. A well-honed practice that develops an internal compass is the only way he can navigate his way amidst uncertainty, chaos, and disorientation. That practice must necessarily be one of gentleness and compassion as much as it is about courage and bravery.

There are very few who are both called to this work of Warriorship and answer the call. At the same time, I know there is either a Warrior in all of us ready to be called, or in none of us, never to be called. With a strong faith in the human spirit, I choose to believe a Warrior spirit lives in all of us, just waiting to be enlisted. That only a select few answer the call isn't because we don't have what it takes to be a Warrior today. Rather, I think there are very few parts of ourselves we're willing to train up to be a Warrior. We strive instead for an overall sense of approval, as if it existed outside of us and unknowingly put off training ourselves up to Warrior-readiness.

Understandably, we get over-focused on the work at hand, and become satisfied when our bills are paid on time, the grass is cut, and we remember to make the kid's lunches before the bus comes. The pull for me to set my most important goals around financial milestones (college funds in the bank, mortgage paid off, retirement account growing and fully funded each year, etc.) is so strong I rarely make time to write much less consider what my deeper calling might be. Social media only exacerbates my procrastination. So, what parts of myself are left to be trained for Warriorship?

When I do make the time, what part of myself do I let be called forth? Why is it not with my whole self? Those who were the ancient Warriors were indeed a very select few. They agreed to step into the battle gear of self-sacrifice with their whole self. I don't think they waited until the affairs of home, family and commerce were managed well enough, as were the internal fears, to sign up and show up for training. When I accepted this, I began to find enough gentleness with myself to let go of what I should be writing and when the book should be finished.

Perhaps today, there are few who are wholly willing to fight the necessary battles to make a difference in their worlds. This book is about discovering that part of ourselves who knows it is called, and gently letting it come forth despite debilitating fears, complete uncertainty and crippling despair. Bringing that part alive begins to influence all the other parts until our whole self is on board – even while we pay our bills, cut the grass, and make the kid's lunches. To be led into the unknown is to be a Warrior. To let our inner Warrior inspire greater leadership in whatever realms we are in, is the clarion call of our times. You're in this chapter, at the top of the compass, after reading all the way around each direction *because you are a brave Warrior.* It's time to accept this is who you were meant to be. Fierce, gentle, brave, and decent.

The Wintery North

The north is often known in the Northern Hemisphere as the place of winter. In native traditions, it is a time when the elders connect with their ancestors and strategize about the coming spring. It is a time to speculate, predict, problem solve, organize, and learn. During the winter, there is often less going on outside. In fact, in the Northern climates many people prefer to stay inside, to make time to read, learn and do more mental things. Metaphorically, we can find our "winter" every day. It is a few minutes of deeper reflection on how we strategize our showing up. By that, I mean how we are present for each conversation and each activity we meet. For me, there is a precious time each morning – my winter – to reflect on my intentions, get mindfully grounded, and nourish my physical body with exercise and good food. This is the time to pause, reflect, and be nourished.

North is the direction of completion and fulfillment of the goals and vision that began in the East. Here there is access to a different kind of knowledge and wisdom. It comes through the East – vision, the South – feminine heart, the West – intellect and envisioning and finally to the North – a time for action. Is completion indeed at hand? Is the Warrior ready?

As the flexibility of the Willow tree is wedded to the sturdiness of the Oak tree, feminine is wedded to masculine. Listening is wedded to action and gentleness is wedded to fierceness. This Warrior accepts the paradox of opposites as a prerequisite for facing the uncertainty ahead.

A Brave Journey

What follows in the next several pages are personal stories of my Warrior's journey and the lessons learned from each encounter with difficulty. This first story is from a time when children could be just children as they learned slowly and even playfully how to become adults. While there has always been a desire to be taken seriously, like we assume most adults are, there hasn't always been such societal pressure to let go of our innocence and childlikeness as there is today. Growing into our wholeness slowly and purposefully, just as a mighty Oak tree begins as a sapling for its first 20-30 years, is what my brave journey has been.

Finding my fierceness of purpose, gentleness of spirit and decency of character took time, patience, and courage. I often wonder if part of this pacing is a window into how we might introduce our own children to their Warriorship. The world today needs them more than ever and ever more urgently.

The tradition of becoming a "brave" was one highly revered among the boys and young men of the summer camp I attended in rural Missouri since the third grade. Each session, the counselors and leaders of the camp would keep their eyes open for young boys who were ready to make the transition into manhood, much like the traditions of many aboriginal tribes. Toward the end of the summer session the boy's camp prepared an American Indian dance session for the girl's camp. I loved learning different steps to the beat of a drum and painting myself with war paint to get ready for the honoring of the local indigenous tribes. Today, and for many years, my childhood camp celebrates and initiates both boys and girls into their Warriorship. I'm grateful for the evolution of thought on just how vital gender diversity of our role models are, and how unconsciously biased we were to have thought only boys could become "braves."

Still, back then it was the boys putting on their performance for the girls. The only stage was a campfire in the woods, ringed by benches, stumps, and rocks upon which the young girls watched in the dark as their "Indians" came out of the woods with solemn faces. After the dancing and fire-lighting displays that went on for over an hour, all the boys sat in an inner circle close to the fire. Two of the "Chiefs" slowly circled. Suddenly they would snatch up one or several of the boys and whisk them off quickly while the Head Chief explained what it meant to be chosen for the experience of becoming a brave to those who remained.

For several years as a young camper, I watched with fascination, longing and chills up my spine watching the older boys get chosen. I began looking out for who was going to be the brave that summer from the time I set foot in the camp. I'll never forget Fred – one of the young men who was chosen when I was about 10 years old. I knew he'd be one of the braves chosen because he had a humble confidence about him and a shy smile for everyone. As I recall, he became very ill from the tests he was put through, and I realized the whole initiation of being a "brave" was far from being a show. He pulled through and passed the tests by forging a deeper relationship with Great Spirit (God in those days), but there were others who failed and didn't become an initiated "brave" as he did. For the next several years, Fred was my hero and I thought of him often throughout the school year.

When I was in middle school a couple of years later, it was my turn. I knew deep in my heart of hearts I had what it took, and I'd be chosen at some point. And still, when the Chiefs snatched me from the circle, it so surprised me that I let out a whoop that frightened some of the other campers, thinking I was in pain. Looking back, I think the whoop came from all my Warrior ancestors confirming that their charge was indeed ready.

That night, my first test was to run as far as I could run, literally until I could not take another step. My guide, a camp counselor, was a long-distance runner and a brave himself many years earlier. He shared with me many practical ideas about running, like pacing myself, breathing evenly, how to embrace the pain of deep cramps and taking care as to how my feet landed on the ground with each step. He went much deeper with his sage wisdom as the steps turned into miles, well into the night. He shared deep truths about man's spirit, about endurance and pain and wholeness that inspired me to find a deeper source of strength than just the muscles in my legs. I think I ran 7 or 8 miles that night, after never having run other than in my physical education classes in school. Collapsing quietly into my bunk so as not to wake my bunkmates, I felt both exhausted and invigorated. I felt Fred's pain and was energized to keep going despite it. Something arose in me that wasn't afraid of the uncertainty that lay ahead. I see this now as the very definition of bravery. At the same time, the needed courage to face my fears gathered momentum in my body long before it reached my mind. I also realized I had only passed the first test of bravehood – endurance, stamina, and spiritual grounding.

The next morning, the rules my guide set out the night before started sinking in. I was given a necklace with three pieces of leather on it to be always worn over the next 2 days. I was to stay silent, honoring a brave's ability to know control, reverence of words and the power of silence. I could make two mistakes, but if the third tally was removed, I would fail.

I inadvertently used the first one to ask an honest question during the next test. Rather than attend the regular camp activities, two counselors who had also been braves in the past, blindfolded me and took me for a long hike into the surrounding woods for what seemed like hours – over rocks, through water, turning and twisting along pathways and through pathless ravines. After a while, they removed the blindfold and said, "a brave relies on more than his memory – he trusts his inner guide and his connection with [Great Spirit.] Now find your way back to camp."

I trusted a power deep within me and everywhere around me, every step of the way. That same spiritual source I found on my run the night before was becoming more familiar. At one point I had a strong urge to cross a fence line, but my mind said that I would be going onto someone else's property and not to do it. The gut-urge wouldn't go away, so after a hundred feet or so of walking by this barbed wire fence, I turned around and asked, "May I cross over the fence?" (The counselors were following about 10 feet behind me the whole way.) Their answer was both heartening and disheartening: "If that is what your inner guide says to do, you may cross the fence, but you will also lose one of your tallies because you asked the question out loud."

What a lesson that I take with me even today. Did I really trust my inner guide to speak for me? What words do I use when I doubt my gut-urges? Not a right or wrong, just an opportunity for observing how an inner dialogue can be a deep body-wisdom knowing or an imaginative story and something that gets in the way. Discerning the difference is a Warrior's moment by moment work. Not surprisingly, after crossing the fence line I found my way back to camp within a relatively short time knowing as I walked back into camp down the gravel road that I wasn't just being tested for the sake of winning a race. I was honing a new and somehow ancient relationship with my inner guide, my kinship with the Creator.

It felt so good to trust myself in this way and to feel so connected to the earth and to Great Spirit. It didn't surprise me to learn later about native people's spirituality being based on a deep, primordial connection with the land, with Mother Earth. Trusting this relationship has been a theme throughout my life. Still today when I feel disconnected, concerned, or confused, simply walking among the trees and grasses brings a satisfying inner knowing that I'd find my way, much like I experienced that day many years ago.

While losing the first leather tally was a disappointment, I knew I had not wasted my words. As I attended a few other camp activities that day I was so attuned to this inner spiritual world that I couldn't speak. Experiencing the power of silence made it much easier for my mouth to stay quiet as well. Here was another life-lesson that had legs: silence was so much more than being quiet – it was being fully present to what is. During those days of not talking, I had my first experience of leaning into silence in a way that it started leaning back on me. To this day, I appreciate the power of silence and let it do much of the “heavy lifting” in my coaching practice.

The final test on the last day was to run one mile in the sweltering humidity of a central Missouri day, with a mouthful of water. At the end of the mile, I had to have enough water left in my mouth to spit it back into a cup. If there was nothing left, I would fail. This test was to prove my ability to gracefully hold on to my inspiration, my abundance, and my equilibrium. I think of all the tests, this was the hardest. Try it sometime! It’s harder than it sounds under normal circumstances, but to run a mile in 100-degree heat and humidity without swallowing or spitting out a mouthful of water at 13 years old seemed superhuman. The mile I ran was a mental one, outside my body. And, paradoxically, I also felt fully part of my body as never before.

That evening, as I felt myself coming back into my pubescent frame, something had shifted. Arriving back at camp after my run, my senses were heightened. I was keenly aware of kids splashing in the pool across the field as if they were splashing me. The sound of a horse’s hooves sprinting lightly around the pasture on the other side of the road were like my feet, sure-footed and playful. The dust from a car driving down the road beside me, leaving a long tail of reddish powder lingering in the air, tasted like the primal earth from whence I was born. Something had changed. When I started the camp session, I was a boy becoming a teenager. When I left camp weeks later, I was a boy becoming a brave man. While that may sound cliché, I know my life was never the same afterward. I think the sense of manhood emerging in me was feeling a part of life itself – being life itself, not just an observer of it. From this place was the ability to face the lost places within myself, to listen for the still, small voices that speak only through silence, and to accept always being tested as an opportunity for resilience. My emerging Warrior was courageous and strong, and powerful, in the deepest sense of those words. Today I'm moved by the power of crossing the boyhood-manhood threshold by means of these native traditions. I wonder what's lost when we, as a society, lose these rituals.

Just as I was riding high on my achievements, I nearly missed completing my brave journey. At dinner that night, I casually asked someone to pass the salt and pepper – as if I had completely forgotten I was still in training and in silent mode. Quickly realizing I had just spoken out loud, I took off my second leather tally. I only had one more and if I lost it, I would fail to complete my training. That night I must have found new respect for the silence that had become a new friend. I knew I would not lose that last tally.

The next morning after breakfast, having passed all the tests, I was inducted into bravehood by the owner of the camp. I really don't remember the induction ceremony but standing on the stage with all the other campers standing and clapping I felt a warmth of accomplishment and I'd never felt before. Remembering it now brings warm tears and a lump in my throat. What I recall most from my "brave" summer was that deep connection with Great Spirit, learning to trust my connection within and understanding that I had something unique to bring to the world. I can proudly say that standing on that stage, I felt deep in my body and spirit that I was life itself. I was chosen to do a great work and I didn't have to be shy about it. This book is my brave labor of love to the world.

A Prophecy of Warriors Arising

Why was my Warriorship formed in a native tradition? Why did I know intuitively that I was a Warrior for some reason? It wasn't until many years later that the gravity of such a claim became relevant. In the Introduction, I shared Chögyam Trungpa's description of the "countless multitudes" of cowards and Warriors who arose. It seems there was a time coming when this rising would be critical. On one level, this rising or awakening is available to everyone to some degree, every day. But on an historical level, I often wonder if this is a unique time for a bigger awakening. Not many data points are needed to consider if now is indeed an inflection point, or an opportunity for a "great awakening" followed by a "great turning" to borrow Joanna Macy's words on what's currently taking place. It's worth noting, the Tibetan Prophecy she received from her teacher, regarding the rise of Shambhala Warriors.

Joanna Macy, a scholar of Buddhism, systems theory, and deep ecology, first learned of this prophecy in 1980 from Tibetan friends living in India. They were beginning to recognize this ancient prophecy from twelve centuries ago may refer to this very time of our people and planet. The stakes we face if this is true are enormous. Does this prophecy refer to the spiritual journey of internal awakening we experience? Or is it an external event that will happen regardless of whether we're ready or not?

Another interpretation, which speaks to the need to integrate our inner and outer worlds was given to Joanna by her friend and teacher Drugu Choegyal Rinpoche. There are several variations of the prophecy available from Joanna herself, all mostly the same, with a few extra words or pauses:

> *"There comes a time when all life on Earth is in danger. Great barbarian powers have arisen. Although these powers waste their wealth in preparations to annihilate one another, they have much in common: weapons of unfathomable death and devastation, and technologies that lay waste our world. And it is just at this point, when the future of sentient life hangs by the frailest of threads, that the kingdom of Shambhala emerges.*
>
> *"You cannot go there, for it is not a place; it is not a geopolitical entity. It exists in the hearts and minds of the Shambhala Warriors. Nor can you recognize a Shambhala Warrior when you see her or him, for they wear no uniforms or insignia, and they carry no banners. They have no barricades on which to climb to threaten the enemy, or behind which they can hide to rest or regroup. They do not even have any home turf. Forever and always, they must move on the terrain of the barbarian powers.*

"...now [is] the time when great courage is required of the Shambhala Warriors. Moral courage and physical courage, for they are going into the very heart of the barbarian power, into the pits and pockets and citadels where the weapons are kept, to dismantle them. To dismantle weapons, in every sense of the word, they must go into the corridors of power where the decisions are made.

"The Shambhala Warriors have the courage to do this because they know that these weapons are manomaya. They are 'mind-made.' They are made by the human mind, so they can be unmade by the human mind. The Shambhala Warriors know that the dangers threatening life on Earth are not visited upon us by some extraterrestrial power, satanic deities, or pre-ordained evil fate. They arise from our own relationships and decisions, our own lifestyles, and habits. They are made by the human mind, so they can be unmade by the human mind.

"So, the time is upon us when the Shambhala Warriors go into training... They train in the use of two weapons... One is compassion and the other is insight into the radical interdependence of all phenomena. And you need both; one is not enough. You need compassion because that is what provides you with the fuel, the mode of force to get you out there to be where you need to be to do what you need to do. And what it consists of, essentially, is not being afraid of the suffering of your world. And when you're not afraid of the pain in your world, then nothing can stop you. Then you can open to it, step forward, act.

"But that weapon by itself is not enough. It is too hot. It can burn you out, so you need the other – you need that wisdom, that insight, into the mutual belonging of everything that is. Interwoven as it is in the web of life. With that wisdom you know that it is not a war between the 'good guys' and 'bad guys.' But that the line between good and evil runs through the landscape of every human heart. And we are so interwoven throughout the web of life that the smallest act, with clear intentions, has clear repercussions throughout that web that we can barely see. But that insight of profound interconnection is by itself a little cool, a little too conceptual, to sustain and keep you moving, so you need the heat of compassion.

"And if you've looked at the Tibetan monks chanting, often you will see their hands doing moving mudras. And as often as not, they are dancing the interplay between this compassion and wisdom… Together these two can sustain us as agents of wholesome change. They are gifts for us to claim now in the healing of our world."[11]

I don't need any more catalyst than this to know I'm on the right journey of Warriorship, or that my journey was formed for a good reason. Honing the weapons of compassion and insight will always serve me well. They contribute to the balance of masculine and feminine energies always in flowing interplay that "can sustain us as agents of wholesome change." While the ability to create change in the outer world

---

[11] This rendition is from the School for Ecocentric Evolution & Design Strategies. See: https://www.jointheseeds.com/joanna-macy-the-shambhala-Warrior-prophecy/

appears circumspect at this point, I refuse to stop my work. In fact, I believe this is the Warrior's work – to bring the training to the deepest parts of my life despite the sadness of being ineffective on a broader scale. Staying in the inner work is the Warrior's inspiration.

How do you know if you're "in your work?" For me it happens on three levels. The first is an intellectual level. I read something like this prophecy, and I see that other thought leaders have seen a need arising for generations. On a heart level, I feel connected to all the relations that have gone before me. I feel the curiosity of their learning. I feel the fear of not knowing just how powerful my vision is. I feel the calling to do more, to keep going and not to give up. And on a body level, I experience the powerful, broad-shouldered stance with a straight spine of a trained athlete or dancer. I also experience the necessary vulnerability of openness in my belly and chest. For me, all three levels combine into the phrase, "strong back, soft front" that describes how my Warriorship lives in all of me. It's a phrase I visit every morning and every time I'm under pressure. The current times demand all our inner Warriors to stand tall and stay open.

Cynthia Bourgeault, a self-proclaimed modern-day mystic who writes about the Christian contemplative and wisdom paths, recently said this about the current times we face:[12]

---

12 From Richard Rohr's October 19, 2020 daily meditation – see www.cac.org

> *"However far any one of us is destined to travel on this wilderness journey, learning to lean into the diminishment, to live with paradox and unknowing, and to celebrate the creativity without dissociating from the pain are all vital survival skills as we humans collectively feel our way into the new beginning."*

Vital skills for a new beginning indeed. So many deep thinkers and thought leaders are naming the pivotal point we're crossing, we no longer have the luxury of just reading or thinking about it. It's our practice of Warriorship that will inform us of how and who we choose to be.

Unstoried Self – an Exercise

One of the most powerful reflections I am deeply inspired by is exploring the "unstoried self." For me, it's one of the practices that keeps me in "Warrior shape" – in thought, heart, and body. By contrast, the "storied self" is the one who picks up all the narratives from the day before – the very same hurts, regrets, anxieties, and fears that I carried around and accepted as true yesterday. The only suffering I experience is caused by the stories I tell myself. This isn't good or bad. It is just part of being human. The "unstoried self" is the native soul that has no weight of stories. Here's an experience I created to experience your unstoried self. See if you feel your strong back and soft front more distinctly afterwards.

Take 5 or 10 minutes to move through the following exercise:

> *Stand upright with your weight evenly spread on each foot. Keep light on your feet, knees slightly bent, head upright looking forward.*
>
> *Now, imagine you're holding a suitcase in each hand. The suitcase gripped by your left hand is filled with evidence of every moment from the day you were born until 1 minute ago. In a secret compartment of this case is a record of all your ancestor's stories, your family tree with all its dysfunction and joy, the trauma of past generations and the secret fears experienced by your mother while she was carrying you as an embryo. Feel the weight of this bag – that bad grade you got in college that still upsets you today; the harsh words you remember all too well from an argument 10 years ago with a loved one; the memory of running out of money in your bank account and not knowing where the next dollar was going to come from. You know the stories that live in this case… feel how they live in you, in this case in this moment. Notice the seductive pull to relive them even now.*
>
> *There is a secret compartment in this case holding trauma, failure and triumph of generations before you. The worst atrocities of war, the signing of peace accords, the horrors and pain of enslavement, the ignorant biases of political and social behaviors, and so on. Even the epigenetics – the actual impact on our genetic make-up of generational trauma – live in this secret compartment. Again, notice the seductive pull to accept as unchangeable and irrefutable, all the stories impacting our life to date, in this compartment.*

Pause and feel the weight of all these stories.

Now, in your right hand, imagine a suitcase filled with every moment that will happen one minute from now until you die. The meeting tomorrow morning you're preparing for and somewhat apprehensive about today; the summer vacation you're planning and really looking forward to; remembering the items on your grocery list you don't want to forget; the goals and visions you have about what's important to accomplish this year, and so on. In this case are also the questions you may or may not consciously verbalize. Have you saved enough money to last you until you die? What will people say about you at your funeral? What will your great-grandchildren, whom you may never meet, hear about you? Will they hear the stories you'd like them to hear? Or will you be remembered for that dumb thing you did, the poor decision you made or the people you inadvertently hurt throughout your life? What about that project that's due in 3 weeks? And the career moves you need to be thinking through. How about that LinkedIn post that will catch the eye of a recruiter who will call you with an amazing job offer? Or the fight you'll have with your spouse that jeopardizes your marriage? Or maybe it's the trip you're planning for the month after you retire? You know the stories that live in this suitcase.

For this moment, feel the weight of everything in this case.

There is also a secret compartment in this case filled with your legacy into future generations. Here are the hopes of your team winning the Superbowl, your child getting into the best college and the promotion you think you'll get in 2 years if you keep working hard. Even more secret or unconscious are the uncertain impacts of climate change, political polarization, and healthcare funding; the recognition of cyclical civilizations that rise and fall (they all do); and the galactic evolution and collapse of galaxies over billions of years.

Notice the weight of these stories – both the hopes and the fears. And pause.

Now, feel your feet on the ground, notice your knees supporting your frame all the way up your spine, your head tilted slightly forward, your arms and shoulders bearing the inconceivable weight of a suitcase in each hand – gripped fiercely, as if you won't know who you really are if you let go of either one.

Notice what it's like to stand here holding these suitcases. This is how we go through 99% of our day.

For just a moment, take a small, but seemingly monumental risk. Set the suitcases down on the ground. Don't worry, you can pick them right back up in just a minute. But for now, just set them down gently and stand up straight and tall. Feel the top of your head inching ever so slightly higher into the sky. Notice this place of weightlessness. This is your unstoried self. There is no need to analyze it, question why you don't know it better or even plan on getting to know it better tomorrow.

Just feel what it's like to put your stories down for a moment.

Pause another moment longer.

Love yourself for taking this time and feeling into your true being.

Now, your unstoried self gets to meet and greet your inner Warrior. With great compassion and patience, notice the suitcases you carry with you so much of the time. Notice whatever thoughts arise – are you surprised? Angered? Ashamed? Just notice how much control and security is present when you hold those suitcases. Before picking them up – and it's only human to do so – ever-so-gently accept there is part of you that craves control of the future and the anxieties that go along with it. And there is part of you that aches for security of knowing and understanding your past. That's okay.

Let your inner Warrior hold this moment. Let it be gentle with all the other parts of you that vie for a voice, a vote, a soapbox.

Beautiful.

Now, notice your heart and your body. Can you stand upright just a little bit more with a corresponding openness to what is? This is the Warrior's relentless work – to gently, but firmly, accept who we are at any given moment and embrace our whole humanity. When we can do that with ourselves, we can more generously to do it with others. Our inner Warrior can be fully present despite the unknowns, the chaos and uncertainty of yesterday, today, or tomorrow. This is the one we've been waiting and looking for. Welcome him. Welcome her. Say thank you for this moment.

Remember, our brain is hard-wired to stay safe, alert and function efficiently. So, we pick back up the suitcases to keep our hard-earned lessons just as close as our wariness about the future. But *how* we pick them back up makes all the difference. Know you can come back here anytime, put down the suitcases to meet your unstoried self, and let your inner Warrior pick them back up with deep compassion and acceptance. When you do this, notice what, if anything is slightly different this time.

Fully in the Body, Fully Present

You just experienced your unstoried, Warrior self. Likely, you also were also fully in your body. I contrast this with being "in our head" since our stories of the past and future live mostly in our mind's eye. There are a handful of times I recall being fully present in my body like this, when time seemed to radically slow down. Perhaps the following examples will spur you to remember the times you've been fully present, fully in your body and fully in your life. This is part of what develops that strong back and soft front.

In high school, I competed as a gymnast. Mastering the art of blending strength and flexibility, the best gymnasts make the hardest moves appear easy and fluid. I worked tirelessly for hours, days and weeks to find my rhythm and flow just to perform a roughly one-minute routine in front of the judges.

Everything came down to those precious moments before leaving the chalk box and heading to the rings. The joyful cheering of my teammates faded. The visualization of my routine was locked in. The last words of encouragement from my coach and his help in steadying me once I jumped up to grab the rings, all blurred into the background. Nothing else existed in that moment – not the hundreds of hours practicing for this moment, not the curiosity of whether I could perform my routine as well as I had the day before in practice, and not the adrenaline pumping through my veins. I was just present, in my body, ready to do what I had done a thousand times before. This is the first time I can remember what real presence felt like. How it was akin to an out of body experience, but fully in my body. Looking back, perhaps it was my inner Warrior coming into his own.

Another time I felt that whoosh of presence was on my horse Noah, loping along a well-known trail on a cool fall day. Saturday chores were finished. The barn stall was clean. The prior week's events were parked. The next week's list of to-dos was off in the distance. And there we were, horse and rider moving in unison through the prairie grasses and warm sunlight, focused only on the utter joy of being there. I was alert, scanning the path ahead for hidden groundhog holes and preparing myself for low-hanging branches that Noah loved to run me under to see if he could knock me off (he had a great sense of humor). But I wasn't overly focused on those things, and they weren't distractions. It was just my beautiful old Appaloosa friend and me, and the world around us, moving in sync.

Similar, but with a different risk profile, was riding my Ducati motorcycle as fast as I could through twisting corners and unpredictable apexes. I had studied the physics of an object needing more power at the rear end to get through a turn and how this was counterintuitive to the tendency to slow down when things get dicey. I was 100% focused on the road in front of me, feeling every thrust of the pistons driving energy into the tires on the road. In the back of my mind, I knew there was a beautiful fall display of color flashing by, the potential for going faster than the posted speed limit and getting a ticket and the real possibility that the mere inches of tire contact with the pavement would get interrupted by a tiny pebble, leaving me in a heap in the ditch or hung up in the trees. And yet, in those moments, nothing else got to take up space in my mind. I was just fully present, in my body, feeling the centrifugal force of gravity and power thrilling me into each corner.

You get the point. When we are fully in our body, we are fully alive. Whether there is real risk, irrational fear, or conditioned hesitation present, they fade just long enough to create a sacred synchronization with the Universe. When do you feel those deeper connections? Immediately after making love? After a good long run? Just before falling asleep at night? Cherish those moments and find a way to tap into the cosmic energy of them. They are a glimpse of the unstoried self and the Warrior within who is called at this time to take a stand and be trained up. Following this calling, even if it makes no sense or appears uncertain, makes all the difference.

The Road Not Taken
by Robert Frost

Two roads diverged in a yellow wood,
And sorry I could not travel both
And be one traveler, long I stood
And looked down one as far as I could
To where it bent in the undergrowth;

Then took the other, as just as fair,
And having perhaps the better claim,
Because it was grassy and wanted wear;
Though as for that the passing there
Had worn them really about the same,

And both that morning equally lay
In leaves no step had trodden black.
Oh, I kept the first for another day!
Yet knowing how way leads on to way,
I doubted if I should ever come back.

I shall be telling this with a sigh
Somewhere ages and ages hence:
Two roads diverged in a wood, and I—
I took the one less traveled by,
And that has made all the difference.

This delightfully poignant poem by Robert Frost has been one of my favorites since high school when I was first introduced to it. We typically know it as a confirmation of taking the road less traveled. It resonates with our inner rebel compelled to make its own way in the world. In this moment, let it call you into the Warrior's path of the unknown, chaotic, and fraught with fear. It is not a road well-traveled or for the faint of heart. But if we are to truly take responsibility for the impact we have on the world around us, we will only make a difference if we follow the road not typically taken. "Knowing how way leads on to way," we may never come back. And that is just what is needed to make all the difference.

Abundance vs. Scarcity

In my experience the tendency to move to action too quickly is ever-present. It is not different for the emerging Warrior. Acting hastily may miss an opportunity for understanding the real motivation and overlook assumptions. When I feel the tug to act hastily, I realize I may be motivated by a sense of scarcity. Time, resources, and adrenaline don't last forever. But if I hold these things as limited, the urgency comes with either a fear or a misplaced, naïve hope. Instead, I can stay longer in the knowing or the unknowing when I feel a sense of abundance underlying my core power. This may be more of a spiritual knowing since what meets the eye is often considered through our lens of human limitation. Love, for example, can be a risk if it isn't received the way we intended. But if the very source of love – love with a capital "L" – drives us, then the risk is mitigated by us not needing to control the outcome. Love, when unconditional, is a boundless power. So, stay here in the abundance longer than you have before. This is key to being with the unknown. Action will come soon enough.

Beautiful Questions

By now in this chapter, you're likely aware of the sacred power of the inner Warrior. I hope you recognize the telltale signs inside of you that know just how important it is to follow. Take a moment to breathe slowly in… and then out. What emotions are evoked? What questions arise for you? Why is any of this important anyway? Beautiful questions. Let them be just that – beautiful questions whose answers and consequent action can stay suspended for a bit longer. Stay with the inner Warrior's presence in you. There is a world of unfolding ahead.

Ready for Battle

Ok, now that you're fully grounded, spent time in reflection of deeper questions and doing real, inner work, you're ready for the more outward battles. If there is uncertainty, doubt and chaos in the inner battles, there is infinitely more in the outer world.

The Lakota Sioux apparently had a tradition of teaching their Warriors to think about competitors with respect and honor. If there was disrespect for their competitors, there was no room for them as a tribal Warrior. The conviction was that competitors exist for personal improvement, or for helping to unearth the jewels within. Only when there is competition could those jewels be seen.

While fiercely fighting to win, Warriorship for the Lakota Sioux included deep respect and honor. Rather than defeating enemies, today's Warrior defeats only the self-limiting beliefs that would keep him from true leadership.

It is interesting to me that the source of the word competition are two Latin words, "com + petere" which means to seek or to "strive in common, strive after something in company with or together"[13]

I believe that today's Warrior must revive that sense of striving respectfully and collaboratively with others to defeat the common enemies of depravation, falling asleep or fighting just to fight. Doing so creates a healthy fitness for bravely facing the complex issues ahead of us. And sometimes, we just need to learn how to stand up for ourselves.

Willing to (get off my horse and) Fight

When I was 21, I had the incredible privilege to live out one of my childhood dreams of being a cowboy. Searching for how to do this, I followed up on a referral from my father to someone who lived in the West and was in the cattle trading business. He didn't know of any opportunities for a college kid to work on a ranch, but the gentleman whose office was across from his in his office building might have a lead, he said. *Note: this is where the Universe conspires with us to co-create the path ahead.* It turns out he owned a ranch in

[13] https://www.etymonline.com/word/compete

Nevada – a huge 350,000-acre ranch. He also had a son who was in college and had worked at the ranch every summer and was looking to do something different this year. We agreed to a job swap – me to the ranch and he to being a runner at the Chicago Board of Trade – and I even got to sublease my apartment to him for the summer. Just like that, my dream was coming true.

There are so many stories of that summer that had a big impact on me. But one of the most poignant ones was trying to fit in with the other cowboys. At first everyone in the camp, including the cook, was curious about this new guy who didn't talk much. Typical stories around the chuck wagon table (yes, we ate every meal in a real chuck wagon) or around the fire in the evenings, were about the best horses they ever rode and the best women they dreamed of "breeding." I was about to graduate from college and had traveled abroad several times. Besides having different views on their topics, or having very little relevance to them, I mostly listened and observed. For a while they thought I might be running from the law and didn't want to give away my identity by sharing anything about myself.

Of the other 7 guys, Thad was the only one who'd ever been out of the state of Nevada, and he was the boss. Pete was a Paiute Indian whose ancestors were hunter gatherers on that land for thousands of years. Bud was a rough Vietnam vet who looked to be straight out of a Marlboro Man commercial, rough, gravelly, and handsome. Kenny was a young, straight-arrow Mormon and a very conscientious cowboy who never drank and rarely swore. Fritz, one of my favorites, was an often drunk and very chatty, sinewy, and leathered cowboy who taught me to roll his cigarettes perfectly, and respect that while cowboys were mostly true to their stereotype of being rough, tough, and ignorant, they were a breed to be admired for their grit. There was also a young craftsman who worked beautifully with ropes and leather and made a "stampede string" to keep my hat on my head. He only stayed for a short time and unfortunately his name has gone the way of the tumbleweed.

Then there was Troy. At 19, his finely groomed handlebar mustache made him the coolest guy in the string of cowboys. His dream in life was to be a beach bum and marry a retired prostitute. He liked to think she'd never leave him for another guy. His ego was a mile wide and an inch deep. About halfway through the summer his curiosity and friendliness turned into animosity, for what I could surmise was no good reason other than I was a threat to his ego. Pete jumped at the chance to test the new guy and started sneaking up behind me while I was riding, and thumping my horse on the rump, causing it to explode in surprise and take off running at a full gallop for what seemed like miles, me hanging on for dear life, trying not to give away that I didn't know what the hell I was doing. *"Pride goeth before destruction, and a haughty spirit before a fall"* (Proverbs 16:18) I thought to myself all too often that summer. I regularly found my rope – a cowboy's cherished tool – either wound the wrong way, making it impossible to use, or found my saddle hanging from a high tree branch.

I knew Troy was behind most of these mostly harmless pranks because he started heckling me and ignoring me. One day, way out in the middle of nowhere, I found myself riding near him without anyone else in sight. Keep in mind, 350,000 acres is over 500 square miles, so it would have been a very long way to nowhere and nobody would have heard me scream if he tried to kill me (even my imagination started playing with me by conjuring up wild stories like I'd read in the Western novels I found in the chuck wagon). He made a snide comment about how I wasn't doing what I was supposed to be doing, even though we were just riding along doing much of nothing.

And there it was – a moment of reckoning. Was I ready for a fight? Is that what it would take to get to the bottom of this? Would I get stabbed or at the very least, get the crap kicked out of me? At that moment, it didn't matter. I needed to be willing to get off my horse and fight. With great bravado in my voice and a hidden panic, I said to Troy, "Fine. Let's just get off our horses and have a go at it" – or something to that effect. In retrospect, the time between the moment the words left my mouth and the time he responded was short. But in that instant, everything moved in slow motion as my thoughts raced between the fear of what I'd do first after getting off my horse and a strange confidence. I'd like to say this was an intentional response from my best self rather than an ego-based reaction to being taunted. In hindsight, it was likely a bit of both.

To my surprise, Troy casually turned his horse away from me, said nothing, and slowly sauntered away, rhythmically swaying left and right in his saddle. After that, all the pranks stopped, from everyone. The boss became a trusted friend and I kept in touch with him for years afterwards.

The lesson learned that day is one I've put into practice many times over the intervening years. Developing a mindset of fearlessness based on an acceptance of circumstances and a sufficient management of the relentless internal stories, mostly based on fear, is the Warrior's journey. The more I practiced, the deeper the calm melted the internal stories, giving them less and less airtime. If there is one trait that survives millennia of Warrior training, I suspect it is fear management.

Several acronyms for fear have come and gone in my life, all bringing me understanding and a different way of holding fear. The first, was likely from a Sunday School teacher sometime in middle school. It was False Evidence Appearing Real. The second came later in my 20's but I can't remember the source. It was Forgetting Everything's All Right. Both write a different narrative on the power of fear by looking at it objectively, as a simple "forgetting" which calls for a healthy "remembering!" Today, while fear still shows up, more often than not, I realize I'm at choice to accept it as real or as a suggestion. If present enough, I can choose not to give too much weight to it. In any case, what I now know is that part of the cowboy's swagger is in his confidence of survival. May I always know the deep-seated power of that swagger. With great power comes a great, sacred responsibility.

Make the Journey Sacred

And, so to complete this chapter, I'll share a beautiful, guided meditation from Sarah Blondin, an inspiring meditation teacher called, *"Make it Sacred."* I first heard it the "Insight Timer" app several years ago. To me it honors each part of the Warrior's adventure as necessarily hallowed, blessed, and sacred. It begins,

> *"Nothing is for certain. It's all a mystery. Even the words I'm saying now are ideas, hopeful perspectives, comforting ideals that help us walk more sure-footed in this great mysterious journey.*
>
> *"There is something however I feel fairly certain is not just a soothing thought but a truth. It feels good and right to lift our faces to the sunrise. It feels good and right to be ultimately guided by our hearts. Something in all of us ignites when we live this way.*
>
> *"I also know that love and attention flow to what we focus our attention on. Our experience changes entirely based on that which we zoom into. And we shift from positivity into morbidity as often as we inhale and exhale. We are in flux. Trying to find certainty when there is none known. How can we quiet our incessant seeking? How can we quiet our quarrelling thoughts when we are living in such an uncontrollable and inexplicable reality?*
>
> *"My answer? Make it sacred.*
>
> *"If nothing is ever known to me, if I live and die never to actually hold anything for certain, I choose to make*

this journey of mine sacred. To make sacred means to hold your life as an exquisite masterpiece. Each moment blessed with the capability to bring your daily doings into the divine space and place of sacred hands.

"... Has something been given to you? Has something cracked open within you? Has joy brought you tears of relief and awakening? Even the gifts, especially the gifts, make sacred. Take a moment to say thank you for what you've been given. To really receive what you are receiving. Grace will grow. Miracles will come like a bolt from the blue if you put your focus on the sacred experience of your life. Lift all you experience into a higher place. It will lift you there too.

"It's indisputable. Make all your life sacred by bringing it into the divine space and place of sacred hands. Make your journey sacred. Illuminate your daily doings. Decide that each offering life hands to you holds the potential to create beauty and acceptance of this mystery unfolding."

The Warrior's journey is, indeed, a sacred, unfolding mystery of finding grace, gentleness, and a bit of swagger. Strong back, open front. Cherish your journey as the exquisite masterpiece it is. Keep going no matter the blustering, winter storms. Congratulations, YOUR inner Warrior has fully emerged! Courage meets compassion in a gentle, graceful balance. You are ready for the battles of life. You are life itself.

NORTHEAST

Oneness

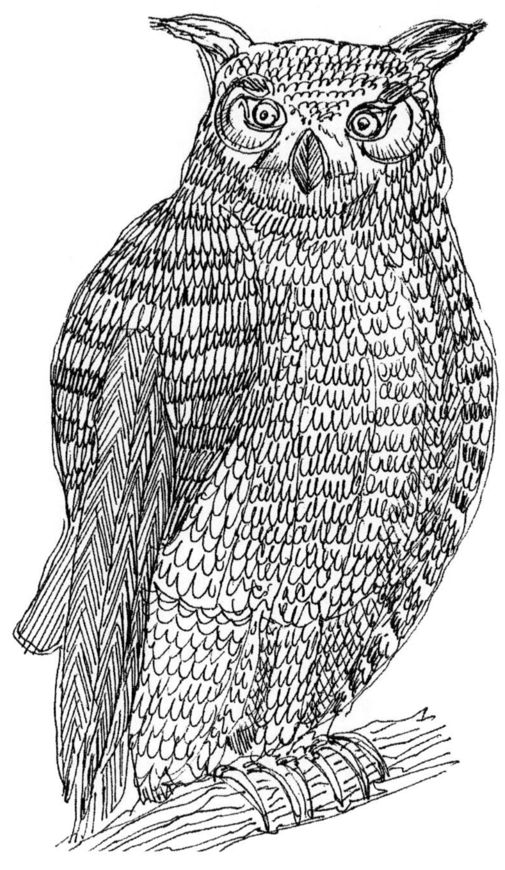

Quotes for the Northeast:

"When we try to pick anything out by itself, we find it hitched to everything else in the universe." – John Muir

"The love of God creates in us such a 'oneing" that when it is truly seen, no person can separate themselves from another person." – Julian of Norwich

"Furthermore, we have not even to risk the adventure alone; for the heroes of all time have gone before us; the labyrinth is thoroughly known; we have only to follow the thread of the hero-path. And where we had thought to find an abomination, we shall find a god; where we had thought to slay another, we slay ourselves; where we had thought to travel outward, we shall come to the center of our own existence; and where we had thought to be alone, we shall be with all the world." – Joseph Campbell

"All things are connected, like the blood which unites one family. Mankind did not weave the web of life. We are but one strand within it. Whatever we do to the web, we do to ourselves. All things are bound together." – Chief Seattle

"Everything is a manifestation of divine radiance. Love rushes everywhere, in everyone, in everything." – Paula D'Arcy

PRACTICE:

Turning to the Northeast – *The Third Owl Appears Proclaiming Oneness:*

Deeply grounded now, balanced in the paradox of polarities, dignified and open.

I know that everything – large, small, known and unknown are interconnected.

I am at one with everyone that comes into consciousness, every blade of grass, every bird's song, every grain of sand.

I am you.

You are me.

There is no separation.

We are one.

Deep Spiritual Integrity

Back in 2008, on my Nebraska land, I remembered my name as Three Owls. The third owl was a theme emerging from my life story told to the fire, of a deep spiritual connection between everything. As I looked back on my life to that point, I saw that spirituality was never far from my thoughts. I loved metaphors, loved the quest to find meaning, depth and value in life and loved the sacred qualities in all things. I was on a quest to sense into a connection with everything through a native integrity to or alignment with Source. This third Owl flies into the Northeast bringing the message of deep spiritual oneness.

Oneness is a concept words can hardly articulate. Still, many beautiful writers over the centuries have helped guide my learning. Thomas Merton, in *Conjectures of a Guilty Bystander,* wrote:

> *"In Louisville, at the corner of 4th and Walnut, in the center of the shopping district, I was suddenly overwhelmed with the realization that I loved all those people, that they were mine and I theirs, that we could not be alien to one another even though we were total strangers… This changes nothing in the sense and value of my solitude, for it is, in fact, the function of solitude to make one realize such things with a clarity that would be impossible to one completely immersed in other cares… My solitude, however, is not my own. It is because I am one with them that I owe it to them to be*

> *alone, and when I am alone, they are not "they" but my own self. There are no strangers... If only we could see each other that way all the time... But this cannot be seen, only believed and 'understood' by a peculiar gift."*

When I first read these words, they reverberated a chord deep inside me. I loved my solitary walks in the woods, but I knew I wasn't alone. I could even feel lonely at times but was always comforted by knowing somewhere deep inside that I was not separate from anything. I knew it was only an illusion covering a more profound truth: *we are all interconnected with everything.*

Perhaps it is the greatest longing we have, to feel this sense of connection in place of feeling separate. Perhaps it is the purpose of the sacred divine to reassure us of this truth. Reassurance is something felt inside. For example, when I look over a beautiful body of water, it makes me smile. I don't know why – it just feels good to see the water reflecting colors of the sky and trees. The Abenaki meaning of Winnipesaukee, a stunningly beautiful lake in New Hampshire, is "smile of the Great Spirit." Ever since I learned that as a child, I sought to understand the spiritual element of physical things. The sunrise I saw out the picture window when I was twelve and shared with my mother, gave us both the sense that all was right with the world on a subterranean level. I know this, and yet I forget every day. And so, we strive to get back to our innate wholeness in everything we do.

Wisdom of Paradox and Polarities

A key element of oneness is an acceptance of that which seems contradictory, an essential ingredient to the Warrior's survival. Oneness means nothing is left out. A paradox is a *seemingly* self-contradictory statement or proposition and appears senseless or absurd from our current perspective. And yet, both are somehow true. It is a paradox that I feel alone and connected to everything at the same time. How often to I forget the opposite of what I can see right now might also be true? It's only when I step back and observe a larger frame that I can begin to see the truth on both sides. This seeing keeps the Warrior alive because it prevents the blind spots and ruts created by over-identifying with only one perspective.

What keeps me from stepping back and observing the larger whole? Fear. Fear that I might have to let go of something dear to me. Fear of letting go of a belief that I'm right. Fear of letting go of a belief that my convictions are the only way of seeing things. It takes a deep humility to accept paradox and yet it is the very thing that is needed for our survival today. If leaders cannot accept paradox, they lead blindly fixated and attached to a paradigm, right or wrong.

There is deep wisdom gained by accepting and leaning into paradox. To grow spiritually, Carl Jung emphasized the need to appreciate paradox. He encourages us to hold the tension of opposites because it *"widens consciousness beyond the narrow confines of a tyrannical intellect."* Being alone and being at one are not mutually exclusive. The point is not to choose one or the other but to stay with the apparent contradiction.

Polarities provide another opportunity to see the power of apparent opposites. The power of a polarity is that it isn't meant to be resolved. Continuing the example of feeling alone and connected, consider how both are needed. When I start feeling lonely, I reach out to others. When I feel deeply connected, I often need to take a few minutes by myself to feel the power of that connection. When by myself too long I begin to feel lonely, and so on, swinging like a pendulum back and forth between deep connection and loneliness. It is in the tension of both being true that I feel whole.

The unstoried self, recognized in the Warrior's North is the lens through which the wisdom of paradox and polarities is gained. Until we stand in this true self, wholeness remains hidden and fear, arrogance and playing small continue to rule the day.

Another realization of the wise spiritual Warrior is the paradox of wholeness and brokenness. Parker Palmer, in his book *A Hidden Wholeness*, writes,

> *"Wholeness does not mean perfection; it means embracing brokenness as an integral part of life."*

The only action required is a gentle, active, and loving embrace of that which chases us and that which holds us together. Why is this so hard to do and why do we relentlessly tear ourselves and each other apart? For me, it's because of another polarity. I am fully awake and then fall completely asleep. Both are needed. But if I over-identify with either one, I put myself in great danger. Either I make everyone else wrong and judge them harshly for being asleep because I'm so "woke" or I judge myself harshly for falling asleep again when so many others are doing good work to stay awake. There is great futility in not accepting paradox and polarities.

Personal Examples

We tend to learn about our wholeness in layers. For me, I can point to three distinct layers of learning about accepting paradox and polarities over the last three decades and I suspect there will be more in the years ahead.

First: when my mother died, my grief was short and intense. About a month after she passed, I took a month and a half off my trading work and traveled to Australia and New Zealand. Early one morning, in deep prayer while witnessing a subtle Southern Hemisphere sunrise, I had a flash of spiritual understanding. In a moment, I saw there were many perspectives on death. Mine was one of loss and feeling alone. I wondered what my mom's perspective might have been. And what about my onlookers who had no idea I was grieving a loss? In that moment, I saw that only my perspective was grieving, or at least feeling the grief I was feeling. My true unstoried self wasn't feeling grief because it was simply present in the now moment. In that instant, I felt my mother's presence as if she was sitting next to me, a feeling that hasn't left me to this day. Sure, I still miss her physical presence all the time. But to my true, unstoried self, nothing really changed. She wasn't physically here, but I felt ever closer to her. To this day, I still feel closer to her essence than I did when she was here over thirty years ago – an unsettling paradox.

Second: when my father and I didn't talk to each other for three and half years, I was never without the relationship with a father. It was just a physical distance and absence that made it seem final. I experienced loss, emotional grief and even anger. But I was never without a father. Holding that paradox gently, with lots of love, forgiveness and humility, the personal relationship slowly healed. I don't think it would have if I hadn't recognized the other side of the paradox that a father/son relationship, albeit separate was always present.

Third: when I was first divorced, I was broken-open to a feeling of darkness I'd never known. In time, I began to see that even that was included in my wholeness. Even the breaking apart of a deep relationship opened a new view to how I was being reassured and taken care of. Oneness didn't get slammed in my face. It gently reassured me in the quietest moments that I was interconnected with everything and was loved unconditionally.

Stuck in any one perspective there is no movement or opportunity for alternatives. Slowing recognizing a different perspective, even a paradoxical one, opened in me the opportunity for softening and healing to take place in each of these three experiences. They opened in me a view of wholeness that emerges through doing my internal healing work.

Richard Rohr says, *"If we do not transform our pain, we will always transmit it."* In his September 17, 2020 post, (see www.cac.org) he says:

> *"Healing is movement and work toward wholeness. Healing is never a definite location but something in process. It is the basic ordinary work of staying engaged with our own hurt and limitations. Healing does not mean forgiveness either, though it is a result of it. Healing is knowing our woundedness; it is developing an intimacy with the ways in which we suffer. Healing is learning to love the wound because love draws us into relationship with it instead of avoiding feeling the discomfort. Healing means we are holding the space for our woundedness and allowing it to open our hearts to the reality that we are not the only people who are hurt, lonely, angry, or frustrated… There is a fierce love that wakes me up every morning, that makes me tell my stories, refuses to apologize for my being here, blesses me with the capacity to be silent, alone, and grieving when I most need to be. You have to understand this is what I mean when I say healing. May all beings be seen, held kindly, and loved. May we all one day surrender to the weight of being healed."*

Wholeness is no longer hidden. Each layer of understanding and healing is a necessary part of the Warrior's journey – the work of bringing our woundedness and subsequent healing outward. This simply becomes part of our on-going work at being human and discovering our true identity.

Love's Deep Embrace

What if divine Love is our deepest identity? If we don't see others as separate from us, then we are made of the same stuff. That "stuff" has sacred roots. That may seem like a stretch in these days of hyper-polarization. It must be time to reconsider the beliefs we hold most dear and see how they either separate us in fear or unite us in Love.

I'm not a religious scholar and I don't think it's wise to take quotes out of the context they were intended for. But my limited understanding of the three major world religions, Islam, Judaism and Christianity, indicates they all teach the importance love loving each other with a sense of wonder. Jesus is recorded in the Gospel of Matthew as saying, *"You shall love your neighbor as yourself."* But he was quoting from Leviticus 19:18 in the Old Testament – the basis of Judaism – which goes on to say we should love *"the alien who resides with you."* The Quran 3:36-37 says, *"do good unto your parents, and near of kin, and unto orphans, and the needy, and the neighbor from among your own people, and the neighbor who is a stranger, and the friend by your side."* If loving each other is a foundational commandment in all the major religions, it must be important. That remains a profound mystery to me! And yet, the ability to love is based on the idea that at our core, we are love. We forget these ancient teachings at our own peril.

Albert Einstein described this peril as a kind of prison. Part of his condolence letter to Norman Salit, March 4, 1950, was reprinted in the New York Times on March 29, 2972. He said the following:

> *"A human being is a part of the whole, called by us 'Universe,' a part limited in time and space. He experiences himself, his thoughts and feelings as something separated from the rest—a kind of optical delusion of his consciousness. This delusion is a kind of prison for us, restricting us to our personal desires and to affection for a few persons nearest to us. Our task must be to free ourselves from this prison by widening our circle of compassion to embrace all living creatures and the whole of nature in its beauty."*

Widening our circle of compassion is an unlocking move to the delusions that keep us from seeing our interconnectedness through Love as our deepest identity. Think about this: to get out of the illusion of separation and loneliness, all we need to do is begin loving what's right in front of us – people, animals, trees, and the beautiful whole of nature. That really isn't too much to ask, is it? Take a moment today to go for a walk outside to feel the presence and connection with and through Love.

The Warrior, at this point in the journey knows Love as our deepest identity. This allows for a wider embrace and connection with all of humanity, nature, and the cosmos.

Without this key component of wisdom, the Warrior is merely a street fighter seeing enemies, foes and that which is outside himself as something to be conquered.

Richard Rohr's daily meditations provide for me a continuing reminder to love as one. Part of his work at the Center for Action and Contemplation (see www.cac.org) is to highlight teachings that support oneness. In a recent daily post, he focuses on one of his Benedictine colleagues, Sister Joan Chittister. He says she, *"calls us to make an unflinching commitment to act with integrity – out of the fulness of our being – not simply our pragmatic, comfortable or fearful selves."* He then quotes her as saying these provocative words in his November 4, 2020 post, *A Call to be One:*

> *"As a people, we are at a crossover moment. It is a call to all of us to be our best, our least superficial... Where in the midst of such polarization and national disunity is even the hope of 'oneing,' of integrating the social with what we say are our spiritual selves?... To be 'one' we don't need one party, one program, one set of policies. What could be duller, more stagnant, more destructive of the soulfulness it takes to create and preserve the best of the human enterprise than such a narrow-minded view of planetary life?"*

Now is the time to get this right. The compass point of Oneness heralded by the third owl is prescient. If we continue to be divided, we will not only fall but collapse. And while even that collapse won't invalidate the reality that we are all interconnected, what suffering might we avoid if we take it to heart now? This state of oneness is a call to unity of consciousness. Some may call it "non-dual realization," or the "unitive state." Whatever name it goes by, seeing the entire cosmos as a creative, compassionate, interwoven whole is an idea whose time has come. It often comes just before the moment of physical death. Why wait if we know it now? Journeying into this unknown realm is difficult territory. But however far we may get, we have everything it takes right now.

I am you.

You are me.

There is no separation.

We are one.

This Owl of the Northeast has spoken her voice of deep, spiritual oneness. She is my reminder that there is a much bigger view always at hand, especially when I feel alone and disconnected from my allies. Who can be an outlier in this purview? With her reminder that I've only forgotten I'm eternally connected with everything else, the cardinal points on the regular two-dimensional compass is complete. While this has been a spiritual journey, it is taken with human feet. And the Warrior is so much more than a human taking a spiritual journey! From here the compass necessarily widens to a third dimension. It's time to put down the two-dimensional maps that brought us here. It's time to look up and to look down for information, guidance, and reassurance.

FATHER SKY

Fully Seen

Quotes for Father Sky:

"The heavens declare the glory of God; the skies proclaim the work of his hands. Day after day they pour forth speech; night after night they reveal knowledge. They have no speech; they use no words; no sound is heard from them. Yet their voice goes out into all the earth, their words to the end of the world. In the heavens God has pitched a tent for the sun. It is like a bridegroom coming out of his chamber, like a champion rejoicing to run his course. It rises at one end of the heavens and makes its circuit to the other; nothing is deprived of its warmth." – Psalms 19 (NIV)

"Oh, Spirit of Father Sky, of the angelic realms, the countless stars of the night remind us that you are vast and beautiful and majestic beyond all of our knowing and understanding. Your light shines upon the earth both day and night guiding our steps. We bless you and ask for your wisdom and blessing here today." – Native American Prayer

"I look up at the night sky, and I know that, yes, we are part of this Universe, we are in this Universe, but perhaps more important than both of those facts is that the Universe is in us. When I reflect on that fact, I look up – many people feel small, because they're small and the Universe is big, but I feel big, because my atoms came from those stars." – Neil deGrasse Tyson

PRACTICE:

Looking UP to Father Sky – *Fully Seen:*

Seeing all—being seen fully and transparently by the Great Spirit of the Heavens.

The whole system is known, honored and purposeful.

Help me to see as I am seen, love as I am loved and surrender into Your arms.

"Our Father, who art in Heaven"

Most Christian prayers begin with this phrase. These words attributed to Jesus evokes reverence for the Creator as a father who is both protector and provider, full of care, a listening ear and love. "Heaven" is the geographical place where this father can be found. Conventionally, heaven has meant up in the sky and many traditions still honor this by pointing skyward when referencing God. While I don't believe heaven is a physical place anywhere up in the sky, the act of looking skyward has a sacred place in the Warrior's practice.

The last two cardinal directions of "Up" and "Down" are three dimensional on the Warrior's Compass and they go together. One cannot exist without the other. Perhaps the beginning line of our prayer could be, "Our Father-Mother within, without and everywhere..." Creation is a feat only accomplished by the coming together of the masculine and feminine. There is giving and receiving, nurturing, and protecting, x and y chromosomes. It is the ultimate point of congruence between male and female. So, when we look to the sky in reverence to Father Sky, we also recognize our feet are supported by Mother Earth. When we look down in reverence to Mother Earth, we also recognize our entire being is seen from above by Father Sky. Father and Mother are permanently entwined into one Creator, Great Spirit, within and without all things.

Right understanding of this relationship is ultimately the basis of what holds the Warrior's Compass in place. By "right" understanding, I mean a paradoxical reverence for spirituality and practical human actions; walking a mystical path with practical feet; being both fully human and fully divine. If we are just humans desperately trying to become spiritual but never really getting there, we're in a futile, unwinnable war with our psyche. It is a magnificent mystery to be both human and divine – a mystery that is to be fully embraced.

The Spiritual Warrior knows to be of this world is possible only as he is also of Spirit. It's okay that this is a paradox – in fact it must certainly be one to embrace its true power. Humankind walks on the plane of confluence between heaven and earth. At the moment of this realization, we embody all the power needed to be of true service because we know we are fully seen.

To Be Fully Seen

To be fully seen is the most basic human craving. To be seen by a creative force then, should be deeply and wholly satisfying. Take a moment to go outside and look up. See the sky in all its magnificence. If the day is light, notice the color of the sky. Notice there is no edge, no border of the sky. Any limitation is only a fantasy of the limitations of your vision. Notice the clouds. Perhaps there is a storm brewing. Above those storms there is wide open, limitless sky. Or it may be dark out. Notice the stars, some bright and some dim. All in their place, night after night. All those beautiful formations are seen only from our vantage point on earth. Imagine what's beyond those stars and what it might be like to look out from their shores. Take in the vastness of the entire sky you can see in this moment and imagine it's trillions and trillions of times beyond that.

Now, imagine that every thought you have, every dream, every fear, everything you've ever done, every hope, every sensation, and every emotion is seen by that sky. Known without judgment. Held with tenderness, protection, and provision. What is it like to be fully seen in this way, by such enormity? Do you feel small? Or perhaps you can imagine feeling big because, as Neil deGrasse Tyson said, "*my atoms came from those stars.*"

Brené Brown, researcher, author, and public speaker, says this about being seen:

> *"Our deepest human need is to be seen by other people — to really be seen and known by someone else. And if we're so armored up, and we walk through the world with an armored front, we can't be seen."*

To be truly seen by Great Spirit, we must begin removing the armor of self-righteousness, judgment, fear, and pride. It is humbling and vulnerable – sometimes even humiliating – to be that open. And yet, for the Warrior to embrace the real power available to all of us, humility is absolutely requisite.

Underneath the humility is a confident sense of self-compassion and self-love. That is how Great Spirit sees us and yet we somehow have a story that to see ourselves with kindness is to be weak or arrogant. Nothing could be further from the truth.

Remember how the Na'vi people from Pandora in the movie Avatar looked into each other's eyes and said, "I see you?" It came from a place of deeply knowing themselves and being able to love from there. When we use the words "I love you," do we really think of seeing the other person deeply, wholly, and unconditionally? To see this way is only possible when we know we are fully seen ourselves. Now, imagine walking down a crowded street and quietly, politely looking at each person and thinking to yourself, "I see you." Every person, plant, bug, thought, past and future is seen by Great Spirit. So, in essence, we channel divine Love when we can let ourselves see others as they are already seen.

Wholehearted Surrender

The true practice of Warriorship is staying awake, which is a life work. There are many avenues for keeping alert, resilient and conscious. For some, religion opens the door. For others, it's yoga, meditation, or peer practice groups. Staying inspired to keep practicing amid the Warrior's requisite sadness at the surrounding conditions isn't easy. But time is of the essence. Since you're reading this chapter now, you know your calling to Warriorship. You also know by now that surrendering into your practice keeps you on track.

Father Sky teaches us about a wholehearted surrender into what is, right now… and right now… and right now. Being seen fully for everything you are, everything you think, and into every molecule of your being, is the magical ingredient to fully embodying this surrender. Wholehearted surrender is largely about letting go of whatever resistance is still arising in you, each moment. It's a full acceptance of the reality – all of it – to what is, here and now.

Letting go is ultimately about getting some distance from the self we unconsciously hold on to, protect and over-identify with. That unstoried self or true self sees best from a distance. You might think of this as going up to the "balcony" of your thoughts or climbing a ladder to see from a different perspective. Letting go of the (small "s") self is likely the hardest thing to let go of, as it is the primary illusion of our lives. And yet, letting go of it is what the Warrior must do.

I used to think that (capital "S") Self was the whole of who we are and marginalized or made wrong the (small "s") self as a human identity I seemed to carry around with me. On an absolute spiritual level this may still be true. But as I'm living here and now in this body, I find it imperative to make peace with my over-identifying with the self I think I am. That's a tough one! But with appropriate distance, we begin to see how connected we are with everything else. This is sacred space. Getting some distance and letting go of my compulsion for attachment to my "self" opens the door to seeing as we are seen.

Moving to Love's perspective is motivated by being drawn by Love or being *"love-drawn"* as Richard Rohr says. And really, isn't it just fear that would keep us from accepting what is? Fear of overwhelm, fear of loneliness, fear of missing out, fear of being let down. Father Sky sees all of it. He isn't afraid of it, disappointed by it, doesn't judge it, and doesn't become attached to it. So why do I? The lesson for the Warrior here is to do the same by wholeheartedly surrendering to what is right in front of us, just as it is. Practicing Warriorship is getting distance from what keeps us small – and embracing it as fully part of who we are.

All Beings are Equal

The events of 2020 cracked me open to the systemic patriarchy embedded in our Western culture. That patriarchy is what underlies systemic racism and sexism. When George Floyd was killed on May 25th, a deep-seated, latent anger came to the surface around the world. That anger had been seething for centuries through slavery, segregation and a dichotomy of inferiority and superiority of one group of people over others. As a white male, I'm embarrassed to say that I was blind to this bias even though I strive constantly to expose it. I have a very, very long way to go to comprehend the unhealed trauma too many people have experienced for generations. But I am building my compassion for it by seeing others as equals. To see them as they are seen.

So much more could be said on this topic and there is so much more work to do. Unless we begin undoing generations of unconscious blindness by seeing as we are seen, it will take many more generations before change takes place. While this is likely an unfortunate path for the general population, the Warrior's path is clear: we must be fiercely courageous in our seeing others as we are seen. That the sky is associated with "Father" isn't meant to be part of the systemic patriarchal problem. Father Sky is vitally connected to and the other side of the coin to Mother Earth.

Father Sky represents true fatherhood protecting, providing for, and seeing over everything in the Universe. Father Sky is the Universe itself, seeing itself as if for the first time. Nothing is left out. Nothing is apart from this seeing. We are part of this Universe, we are in this Universe, and perhaps more importantly, the Universe is in us. To know this is to also hear a thunderous rejoicing at its recognition. The language of the Psalmist quoted at the beginning of this chapter, echoes this all-embracing view:

> *"In the heavens God has pitched a tent for the sun. It is like a bridegroom coming out of his chamber, like a champion rejoicing to run his course. It rises at one end of the heavens and makes its circuit to the other; nothing is deprived of its warmth."*

Help me to see as I am seen, love as I am loved and surrender into the arms of Great Spirit, the all-seeing, all-knowing divine Warmth.

MOTHER EARTH

Sustenance of Life

Quotes for Mother Earth:

"Those who contemplate the beauty of the earth find reserves of strength that will endure as long as life lasts." – Rachel Carson

"Oh, Spirit of Mother Earth, you support us each day, welcoming our roots deep in your heart. You nurture and guide us finding sustenance and support. Help us to give thanks always for your bounty. We bless you and ask for your wisdom and blessing here today." – Native American Prayer

"Kinship with all creatures of the earth, sky and water was a real and active principle. In the animal and bird world there existed a brotherly feeling that kept us safe among them... The animals had rights – the rights of man's protection, the right to live, the right to multiply, the right to freedom, and the right to man's indebtedness. This concept of life and its relations filled us with the joy and mystery of living; it gave us reverence for all life; it made a place for all things in the scheme of existence with equal importance." – Chief Luther Standing Bear

PRACTICE:

Looking DOWN to Honor Mother Earth - *Sustenance of Life*

Holding hands outward in a welcoming gesture. Thank you, Mother Earth, for providing the very breath of life for every bug, tree, flower, seed, bird, animal, plant, and being.

We are all blessed by your generosity, guidance, and abundance.

Generosity and Abundance

Imagine picking up a handful of raw earth soil right now. Even better if you can go outside and find a bare patch of earth, dig up a bit of soil and look deeply into it. Bring your nose close enough to breathe in deeply the humus, earthy richness. Remember that smell of clean earth after a warm rain? That soil is the culmination of millions upon millions of years of life cycles. Nutrients that allow seeds to germinate. Moisture that recycles from aquifers below the ground to rivers, lakes, and oceans to clouds and rain. The very body and bones of every plant, insect, bird, tree, animal, and human that ever populated the earth. All minerals from gold to diamonds, coal to uranium and crude oil to iron. All in that handful of soil. And what does this generous giver of all life ask for in return? Nothing. This is the hallowed ground on which the Warrior lives and dies.

As we begin to understand the generosity of this precious resource, perhaps we will also begin to accept its vast love for us. I think this is why we often use the term "Mother Nature" and "Mother Earth" to describe planet earth. Anthropomorphizing this being into a goddess is appropriate! She is indeed the most resplendent source of generosity we can ever know.

Take a moment to take in the consistent abundance of that handful of soil. We owe every breath we take to the ongoing life-giving processes of the earth and everything that grows in this soil. Our clothes are spun from her riches above and below the surface. Our machines are crafted from her ore and our buildings are glassed over from her sand. Everything we can see, and everything we will ever see around us, comes from the generous offerings of Mother Earth. It's time to come home to all that is, to appreciate and fall deeply in love with the source of all life.

When we walk through life with a sense of abundance, we make decisions and speak our words with confidence and poise. When we come from a place of scarcity, we play small, hoard our resources, and make decisions from a place of protection. Thinking every day of the earth's one-way gift of abundance, one which asks nothing in return, nourishes our decisions and our words. It creates in us an urge to take a long-view perspective of stewardship of these resources. Mother Earth plays the long game. So must the Warrior.

Unfortunately, we've long been misguided by the King James Version of Genesis 1:26-28: *"And God said, Let us make man in our image, after our likeness: and let them have dominion over the fish of the sea, and over the fowl of the air, and over the cattle, and over all the earth, and over every creeping thing that creepeth upon the earth."* The word "dominion," or in the original Hebrew "radah," is taken to mean "to rule over" or quite literally "to dominate." But there is a sense of force in this translation I don't see in the context of God making man in Her image. Is God a forceful, dominating presence or an abundant, graceful one? If God is forceful and dominating, then Her image would be forceful and dominating. Sometimes we as humans are indeed dominant.

But I think there's more to what the author intended in this beautiful description of creation. Could it be that this description is about us as spiritual beings as well? I think we are something more than just human creation. Even if we're not, I believe we are something more than just an ego wired to dominate over others.

How we answer this question of what we are at our core – as the image of the Creator – seems key to how we act toward the earth's precious resources. My sense is that at Her heart's core, the Creator embodies a strong element of love, just as parents, in their heart of hearts, love their offspring. They steward their children's growth, maximize their skills, and support them becoming independent adults. At risk of sounding preachy, wouldn't it make sense to treat the earth with the same sense of love, reverence and stewardship as parents do for their children? And at some point, later in life, as children do for their parents? I choose to say a resounding YES every day when I appreciate the abundance of Mother Earth.

Falling Asleep – or Waking to Her Gifts

We live in a time when too few take the time to recognize the preciousness of the earth's resources. Those who work the land to produce agricultural products too often take a short-term perspective by dumping fertilizers on what was once fertility itself to boost production – at the expense of longer-term viability. Too most others, the gifts of the natural world are removed from our daily experience short of a few blades of grass or a stepping in a rain puddle when crossing the street. We rush from one thought to the next, one activity to the next, without pausing to absorb the beauty and abundance all around. We buy groceries from the story, having no idea of the time-honored process of cultivating plant and animal growth. In effect, we sleep-walk right past this most amazing display of life.

Appreciation must be met with action, otherwise the consequences are dire. In "*The Soil's Story is the Story of Us,*" authors Annie Leonard and Tom Newmark write,

> *"Thousands of years of taking have caught up with us—and our soil. Approximately 40% of agricultural soils worldwide are degraded or seriously degraded; we lose an estimated 36 billion tons of topsoil every year. Scientists warn us that we only have about 60 years of productive soil left. What will happen when the Earth has lost all of its soil and can no longer produce food? While this is a dire future, it doesn't have to be our destiny. It's time to act. And the solution is under our feet... If enough of the planet's arable acreage were converted to what [is] described as 'regenerative' agriculture, we could draw enough carbon dioxide from the atmosphere and mitigate climate change... composting can build community social and economic resilience. For example, in Manila's barangays, or small neighborhoods, in the absence of regular wasted collection, the Mother Earth Foundation organizes residents to compost organic material, [which is] used in potted gardens... Figuring out local composting systems requires us to come together to solve problems*

> *that affect us all, and we're going to need a strong sense of community to guide us through our soil and climate crises... The story of the soil is the story of all of us and it spans eons."*

It is now time to wake to the urgency of caring for our earth. Sadly, it may be beyond an urgency, but there is no time like right now to begin with some action like composting, re-using, and consuming less. It's time for spiritual activists to become earth activists. Yes, this sounds highly liberal, granola and hippie to some. But I can no longer tolerate my fear of bringing it up because I may rub someone the wrong way or insinuate that someone else's freedoms are more important than our collective survival. I'm willing to sound alarmist by saying the time to deal with climate change may have already passed us by.

And I fail miserably taking in the seriousness of the current emergency every day. I forget to fix something rather than throw it away. I turn up the heat instead of putting on a sweater. I drive to the store for one forgotten ingredient. And so on. This is not meant to be a soap box from which to decry the evils of capitalism or religious doctrines that have led us astray. It is meant to keep me awake to what is going on right under my feet every moment of every day. The earth is supporting me, and I owe it to Her to say thank you by being a good steward of the resources we have. I say thank you by listening and letting nature guide my actions and reflections.

Life's Guidance and Power is in the Trees

There was a large Burr Oak tree in my backyard growing up in the suburbs of Chicago. I was compelled, perhaps from a naturally childish impulse to be in and with natural things, to climb up and into this tree frequently. As I did so, I got to know her seasons and her consistent reach for sunshine. Every branch was designed for maximum access to the light that fed her, and it so happened, perfectly designed for climbing. Sitting way up toward the top of this tree, I could see the whole neighborhood. I'd often sit there daydreaming while inspecting the buds, leaves and acorns. While perhaps not based on scientific inquiry, I felt my curiosity came from some kinship with the natural world.

When my family moved across town to a bigger piece of property and built our dream house, I found another welcoming Oak and built a platform large enough to spend hours just living up in the air, in the middle of the woods. Once, a racoon came along, likely as surprised to see me on "her" platform as I was to see her on "my" platform. We eyed each other inquisitively for several minutes – from about 3 feet apart – before she scampered around me to another branch. I figured she was satisfied that I wasn't a threat or a menace to her endeavors whatever they might have been, because I was willing to just be still. This experience encouraged my connection with what was around me. I watched deer browse the flora just below me without being seen. Skunks waddled through the woods without noticing my presence. The winds passed through me, on their way to nowhere. I was part of the flow of life by seeing things from up in my tree.

Today, on my daily walks, I often pause by another Oak tree long enough to let it become my teacher. I ask whatever questions come to thought that challenge my limited perspective and prompt a long-view, like:

- *How is the bark on this tree trunk viewing world events at this moment?*
- *How are these branches responding to my grief, anxiety, or frustration?*
- *Do the leaves at the tips of those branches experience fear or loss?*

The guidance I receive doesn't come through analysis or process. It is a heart-sense of abundance, confidence and looking forward with great expectation, unfazed by temporary disruptions. Despite destructive high winds that may knock down branches or fire that may burn off leaves or the entire trunk, the march toward growth and rebirth is constant. This is the source of the Warrior's true power and focus on the long view. Mother Earth teaches this lesson repeatedly. Am I willing to listen?

When I let the power of abundance and growth guide me, I can act with humility and servant leadership. By developing a deeper affinity with Source, the Warrior inherits power that does not corrupt. The short-sighted temptation to lead from greed is seen as a distraction to the real work ahead: being a valiant steward of my resources.

Grateful and Awake

Take an hour this week to reconnect with Mother Nature, to offer Her your awe and wonder. I suspect you know how it feels to call home to your human mother just to say, "I love you" and hear back something like, "oh, my darling, I love you!" Do you know that is what Mother Earth is saying at every moment?

> *"You're loved. I provide for every breath you take and every bite you eat. I am abundance and generosity itself."*

Can you hear that voice as you walk through a forest, along a beach or through a city park? If you can't get outside right now, find a picture of a tree or a cloud formation, and behold its wonder and beauty.

Speaking of wonder, have you ever seen pictures of snowflakes or icicles against a black backdrop? Oh my – they are a work of divine art and each one uniquely gorgeous. And while looking at ice, look up in the trees and see the winter birds roosting. And the sun setting in the background. And, and, and. In his book, "*Wonder: When and Why the World Appears Radiant,"* Paul Fleischman writes this wonderful paragraph:

> *"In order for this moment of wonder to have occurred, here I sit in my office, as my planet rushes through space at about five hundred thousand miles per hour (there are many motions in this approximation: the Earth revolving around the Sun, the Sun moving in the Milky Way Galaxy, the galaxy sweeping forward*

with expanding space), through the caverns that are (at least) fourteen billion times six trillion light years wide, my planet having given birth to life some three to four thousand million (billion) years ago, and having created in that long interval about fifty billion species, and having covered itself with oxygenated plant-breath, and having ushered in oxygen breathers, and having elaborated in the play of life over the most recent hundreds of millions of years complicated mammals, who have increasingly complex minds, all of this swirling aloft in my one hundred trillion cells, one hundred trillion informatic DNA threads, septillions of ATP's and thousands of other smart molecules, containing octillions of atoms whirring with coordination and precision and whizzing accurately among themselves across uncountable nano-gaps, while creation and destruction bring life and death to me with their roughhouse game… One moment of icicles and birds pours out of the cosmic fountain. One moment of awareness of icicles and birds is more, and different, than everything. But there is no resting place, and the scene moves on.

I went into a doctor's office several years ago to find a picture of a redwood forest covering the entire wall behind his desk. It was magnificent to behold its hues of leafy greens and mahogany reds. I asked the doctor why he chose this beautiful mural on the wall and his answer inspired me to get outside at least once a day from that point on. He said that just looking at a picture of a tree causes your stress hormone levels, called cortisol, to go down by about 10%. Imagine, he said how much you naturally feel less stress by taking a walk amongst live trees? For a doctor who is in the practice of helping to heal people, this wasn't just happenstance. He knew people began to feel better just by being in his office before he did any diagnostics.

What might be different if you really accepted this abundance? Rather than find all the reasons things aren't going your way, all the places you're bumping into dead ends and feel the effects of scarcity and lack, just turn toward Mother Earth, open your senses, and say thank you.

Kristi Nelson, at Gratefulness.org said:

> *"When we allow ourselves to fall in love with the Earth in all her splendor, we strengthen our bonds of connection. We allow ourselves to experience the great fullness of our emotions at how inextricable we are from the Earth's perpetual flow of gifts, recognize how much and how often we take them for granted, and grieve the losses our Earth and all her creatures are suffering daily at the hands of our civilization. Gratefulness invites us to heal our disconnection, live in greater celebration, and strengthen our place in the rightful relationship of reciprocity with the natural world."*

It is time to come home to all that is, to appreciate and fall deeply in love with the source of all life. Here is solid ground from which to face the complexity, chaos and conflict caused by ignorant human impact. It is indeed an unknown place to confront. We have no idea whether future resources may sustain or disappoint us. To live sustainability is our gift to future generations. As Rachel Carson so eloquently said,

"Those who contemplate the beauty of the earth find reserves of strength that will endure as long as life lasts." It is my deepest hope that life will last a very long time. I'm going to do my part by summoning those reserves of strength and stay alert to and connected with the beautiful source of all life, Mother Earth.

CENTER

The Secret Sits in the Middle

Quotes for the Center:

"We dance round in a ring and suppose, but the Secret sits in the middle and knows." – Robert Frost

"Peace enters the human soul when it recognizes the oneness with the universe and that the Creator dwells in the Seventh Direction, at the center of the universe, which is everywhere and within each person." – Black Elk

"The way upward and the way downward are the same." – Heraclitus

"Stay in the center, and you will be ready to move in any direction." – Alan Watts

"We shall not cease from exploration
And the end of all our exploring
Will be to arrive where we started
And know the place for the first time.
Through the unknown, unremembered gate
When the last of earth left to discover
Is that which was the beginning;
At the source of the longest river
The voice of the hidden waterfall
And the children in the apple-tree
Not known, because not looked for
But heard, half-heard, in the stillness
Between two waves of the sea." – T.S. Eliot from the Four Quartets

"We are the ones we've been waiting for." – attributed to a Hopi Elder

PRACTICE:

Soft gaze into the Center - *The Secret Sits in the Middle:*

Left hand over right fist, two inches below the navel – this is my center.

I notice where I stand is at the confluence—the co-incidence of heaven and earth. This is the place where humanity exists, connected above and below, supported, and seen, never alone, never disconnected.

And so, I bow to the Center where the perfect point of alignment exists.

Gathering in all the energy from the Earth below...
Gathering in all the energy from the Sky above...

I bring it up through my body while breathing in – and pushing my breath out as I raise my hands to the sky.

Then bringing all the energy from the Sky above while deeply breathing in, pulling it down through my body – and pushing my breath out loudly, giving it back to the Earth.

Rubbing both fists on my lower back (kidney area) 3 times and with a loud "Haaa," releasing all energy into the Earth.

I take in nothing extra. I am complete and have everything I need today.

I rest in the Center of the compass, fully grounded, fully prepared, fully accepting of what is.

Centering at the Center

The final direction on the Warrior's Compass is the Center. Imagine the internal mid-point in a gyroscope, around which the wheels can spin but the center remains still. This is the center of this compass, where we are now, both in this book and metaphorically in this time of our world. All directional headings reach outward and back inward from this one point. In nature and in much of sacred art, the circle unfurls from a central point. Think of how a fern frond opens beautifully and majestically outward from an invisible center. On this journey around the "sacred hoop," the Warrior's Compass, to each cardinal direction, we come back to the beginning, the center. It's a place we now know well: open, at ease and allowing what is with a strong back and soft front – and know it as if for the first time. The messiness of daily life goes on all around us and yet, at here our core, we remain centered and grounded, again and again and again. It is our time to claim our place in the center of every decision and every action.

In much of sacred literature and in stories about the hero's journey, a seeker becomes transformed in the process of entering life's winding labyrinth of unknowns and uncertainties. The journey naturally winds its way into the center, into the depths of truth and life itself. In this place, the seeker often realizes they are always at the center of their universe. And, as the hero's journey goes, they must necessarily carry their learned gifts and intentions back out into the world, just as the path in a labyrinth winds its way back out to the edges. American author James David

Audlin writes in his book, *The Circle of Life: A Memoir of Traditional Native American Teachings,*

> *"Wherever we are, we are at the center of the Universe... The horizon around us reminds us of that fact. No matter how far we go, we still see the edge of the visible Earth equidistant from us in all directions. No matter how far we go, the Sky still stretches over us."*

We never really leave the center, but we forget this truth all the time. The center is where we operate from all the time even when we don't know it is the place of our true power. No matter how far afield we believe we are, the Creator, Universal Truth, Father Sky still see us right where we've always been. Right here. Right now.

Most fields of practice point to the center of our body as that place of true power. Getting "centered" is a common term in many practices. In Japanese martial arts our energetic center is known as "hara." In Chinese it is known as the lower "dantian," loosely translated as an elixir field. It is an energy center also known as Ki, Chi or Qi. This place is considered a store house of energy. There is no place to go, no beginning and no ending here. It is not a gateway to something or somewhere else. It is simply the center.

In the physical body, our energy center is a point just below our navel and inside our body, closer to our spine than our belly. Focus your attention on this point inside your body now. As you take a deep breath in, let the air go right down to this center point. Exhale slowly from this place. Do this two more times. Do you feel that place of being grounded, like your body, heart and mind are all in alignment? Like water flowing around rocks in a stream, any other thoughts that arise, simply pass by without getting hung up, being thrown off, or complaining. In this place, alignment already is and is effortless. There is no place to go or get to.

Going through all directions on the Warrior's Compass is one of many centering practices all of which aim to bring us back to a recognition of this place. Think of a time in your life when you felt centered and grounded. Find the memory of that time as a place in your body now. Often, it's in your core. Like a tree that has roots deep in the ground and a trunk and branches reaching toward the sky, the center is that point where the trunk meets the earth and reaches both directions at the same time. As Heraclitus says, "*the way upward and the way downward are the same.*" Both directions are life-affirming, and both are needed for sustainable growth.

The beauty of this point in our center is that it doesn't try to change any of the messiness or darkness of our experience. It just lets it be. Here, you are at the center of your true nature. You are completely open and at ease. From here you can speak your truth without fear or judgment. As Black Elk says, "*the Creator dwells [here], at the center of the universe, which is everywhere and within each person.*" Again, nowhere to go, nowhere to be, nothing to fix or adjust. Just a place to be with what is – including collapse, complexity, chaos, and fear.

Unaffected by External Circumstances

Paradoxically, this is the both the culmination of our life work, and the point from which each day starts anew. We begin where we started yesterday, with a clean slate. Externally, life continues to be a series of ups and downs, joys and sorrows, wins and losses. History is filled with traumas like the holocaust, slavery, cataclysmic weather events, world wars, corrupt dynasties, self-serving czarist regimes, and polarizing politics. From the center, the future anxieties and past traumas can all be held more lightly.

There will be more discouraging news. There will be fearful odds that the human species will not survive. The sense of impending collapse will provoke fear and disgust. The disheartening conflict, disruptive chaos and overwhelming complexity will not go away. They will only grow. This is what is. But the "*Secret sits in the middle and knows*," says Frost. I believe that secret is our truest nature, our True Self, knowing, unchanging and untouched by external circumstances. This is why we need not hope or fear for ourselves to be anywhere else. Fiercely and courageously, we move to action armed with insight and compassion, with a strong back and an open front. We are ready. We were born for this moment, to do the work required of us in this time.

Perhaps it is this knowing that allowed Anna Waring, a Welch poet and hymn writer, to pen these lines to one of her best-known hymns, "*In Heavenly Love Abiding*" in 1850:

"In heav'nly love abiding,
No change my heart shall fear;
And safe is such confiding,
For nothing changes here.
The storm may roar without me,
My heart may low be laid,
But God is round about me,
And can I be dismayed?"

I remember well humming and singing this hymn from my Sunday School hymnal during my darkest, fear-filled times growing up and through early adulthood. Times when I didn't know where to go or what to believe. The poet's voice was speaking something I knew to be true deep within my core, at my fearless center: the whirling and roaring storms of life don't change who I am, who I know myself to truly be. Today, these words re-ground my resolve not to be dismayed even in the sadness and lack of certainty ahead. I believe it also re-affirms that we are a spiritual being having a human experience. It's the only conclusion I can trust. And the mystery of it all remains, fulfilling the paradox of being at once in the center and everywhere at the same time.

Why this Matters

Few leaders today have the necessary skills to survive the uncertainty, complexity, and unprecedented chaos ahead. What's ahead is clearly unknown. The events of 2020 proved this point. While the entire world faced a pandemic at the same time, few did anything to allay the fear and disorientation of the rest of the world. In fact, many leaders looked to how the circumstances affected them first. They took the short view, and we are suffering as a result. In the next decade, this lack of leadership will only exacerbate the calamity and uncertainty. Other leaders found their center and looked for opportunities to commit to a long-term vision, recommit to their core values and find a deeper empathy for their employees, customers, and community.

In 2010, McKinsey published a study entitled, *"How Centered Leaders Achieve Extraordinary Results."* (Who knew that the ability to be "centered" would be so needed ten years later?) The study surveyed nearly 2500 executives representing all regions, industries, functional specialties, and tenures. Respondents indicated their level of agreement with statements representing various dimensions of a leadership model. Answers were then aggregated into degrees of mastery of each dimension. There were five dimensions identified as "centered leadership:"

- **Meaning** (happiness, strengths, and purpose)
- **Managing Energy** (minimizing depletion, restoration, and flow)
- **Positive Framing** (self-awareness, learned optimism and moving on)
- **Connecting** (network design, sponsorship, reciprocity, and inclusiveness)
- **Engaging** (voice, ownership, risk taking and adaptability)

Perhaps this list can be a quick guide for all warriors seeking to find their center. Which ones do you do well? Which ones are a stretch for you? The study found that "*leaders who have mastered even one of these skills are twice as likely as those who have mastered none to feel that they can lead through change; masters of all five are more than four times as likely.*" The impact of centered leadership through a time of disruption and change cannot be underestimated. Like working all the way around the Warrior's Compass, the effects of leading from your center are greater presence, quicker resilience, and a timeless sense of belonging – despite all evidence to the contrary.

By cultivating the beautiful dignities in each direction of the Warrior's Compass, leaders can frame challenges more constructively, give a sense of meaning and direction to people around them, leverage emotions into greater empathy and redefine success. Energy is more sustainable and resilient. Sadness does not deplete. Success, redefined, includes a much broader based of stakeholders (beyond just financial shareholders). It matters that business, political, community and religious leaders find a way to be centered, and lead from that place. It matters now and the urgency isn't going away.

In fact, this is precisely the time when the prophecy of the warrior's arising is needed. From the introduction to this book, here again are the words of Chögyam Trungpa in *Shambhala: The Sacred Path of the Warrior*:

> *"When fear and doubt occurred*
> *Towards the confidence which is primordially free,*
> *Countless multitudes of cowards arose.*
> *When the confidence which is primordially free*
> *Was followed and delighted in,*
> *Countless multitudes of warriors arose."*

Will you let the Warrior within you arise from your center? Or will you continue to be ruled by fear and doubt, informed by the events around you? The Warrior of True Self will always be here. Sink into your center and feel your fierce courage arising. Remember the prophecy given to Joanna Macy (see North chapter):

> *"There comes a time when all life on Earth is in danger. Great barbarian powers have arisen. Although these powers waste their wealth in preparations to annihilate one another, they have much in common: weapons of unfathomable death and devastation, and technologies that lay waste our world. And it is just at this point, when the future of sentient life hangs by the frailest of threads, that the kingdom of Shambhala emerges.*

Make no mistake. The time has come for the Warrior in you and in me to emerge well-trained, well-centered and ready to make a difference. The urgency of the prophecies come through the words on this page with an armload of love, compassion, and courageous resilience.

I'm reminded of Ursula Le Guin's comment, quoted on the first page of this book, that, *"the only thing that makes life possible is permanent, intolerable uncertainty; not knowing what comes next."* This matters most right now because not knowing must become our way of traveling. How we travel during *intolerable uncertainty*, with our back straight and strong and our front open and curious, makes all the difference.

Beginner's Mind

To face the brutal realities ahead with a Warrior's strength of insight and warmth of compassion, openness, and curiosity, I think one more skill is needed. This one can only be refined and honed in the Center. It is the Zen concept of "shoshin" or beginner's mind. Zen mind is looking at everything as if for the first time, or from a place uninhabited by preconceived ideas. Imagine the first time you were going to kiss someone – the sense of wonder and eagerness you experienced with a heart aflutter. Or the feeling of opening a gift on your birthday as a loved one eagerly watched. What if that same mindset could precede a reading of the news each day? Might you consider what's going on with more empathy for the people involved? Would you consider more options rather than shrug off one more disappointment of hearing the same thing over and over again?

Beginner's mind is a life-long practice. It's taking one thought at a time, as if for the first time. It's falling down eighteen times and getting back up nineteen. It's letting go of being an expert and sometimes even common sense. It's recognizing that while you might have seen, heard, or done something a thousand times, this time is the first time you've heard it, seen it or done it at this moment in time. It's a way of traveling through complexity and chaos with the *only thing that makes life possible,* not knowing.

Over many years, I've challenged myself to savor this kind of uncertainty, especially when just the notion of not knowing makes me feel downright nauseous. Just when I need to know something the most, right there is the opportunity for savoring not knowing, lingering uncomfortably on each discordant note. This is what is. This is where we are in our world. What if we were perfectly designed by the Creator to be right here, right now at this place in time? If we were born at this moment in history to serve our fellow human beings in this way?

What are you a Warrior for?

Throughout the Warrior's Compass, the focus has been on practicing your warriorship, honing the skills of visioning, healing, teaching, and standing strong. And it now bears asking, "what are you a warrior *for?"* as you stay with what is. In what direction will you now leverage your skills? Many people will answer this differently depending on the challenges and circumstances they're called to meet. I've purposely left this question open until you've mastered your warriorship skills. Now it is time to go out and do your work in the world.

But wait… what of human flourishing amid uncertainty and chaos? Is that even possible? Does the human spirit have what it takes to make it through our trying times? Present circumstances often leave me distraught and sad. But from this place of being centered, I'm called again and again to focus my sights on the best of humanity and it's right to flourish. Yes, *flourish.* From my center, I take a courageous stand for flourishing leadership amid uncertainty. To me, this means the best of leadership – the best of humanity – is called forth as an imperative response to the crisis at hand. The best includes finding meaning and purpose in our work, staying fully engaged and in flow when we're most tempted to fall asleep, and maintaining a strong sense of trust, support, and connection with others despite evidence to the contrary. This is the secret that sits in the middle.

The secret is no longer hidden. It is revealed as an imperative, if not overdue, call to action. It seems a fitting place to end with one last prophecy, apparently written by an unnamed Hopi (southwestern American Indian tribe) Elder in 2000. While anything attributed to an unknown, unnamed source is suspect, the message here is unmistakably suitable for the current time and too great to ignore:

> *You have been telling people that this is the Eleventh Hour, now you must go back and tell the people that this is the Hour. And there are things to be considered…*
>
> *Where are you living?*
> *What are you doing?*
> *What are your relationships?*

Are you in right relation?
Where is your water?
Know your garden.
It is time to speak your truth.
Create your community.
Be good to each other.
And do not look outside yourself for your leader.

Then he clasped his hands together, smiled, and said, "This could be a good time! There is a river flowing now very fast. It is so great and swift that there are those who will be afraid. They will try to hold on to the shore. They will feel they are being torn apart and will suffer greatly. Know the river has its destination. The elders say we must let go of the shore, push off into the middle of the river, keep our eyes open, and our heads above the water.

And I say, see who is in there with you and celebrate. At this time in history, we are to take nothing personally, least of all ourselves. For the moment that we do, our spiritual growth and journey come to a halt.

The time of the lone wolf is over. Gather yourselves! Banish the word 'struggle' from your attitude and your vocabulary. All that we do now must be done in a sacred manner and in celebration.

We are the ones we've been waiting for.

My leadership and your leadership are needed now. With deep empathy, fierce compassion, and keen insight, our warriorship is called to let go of the shore, take nothing personally and gather ourselves. Those we have so desperately been waiting for to lead us, will only arise from *within* us. That is a cause for great celebration, even if amidst a deepening sadness – a paradox I'm willing to hold.

A Second Look

Sometimes, our first look at something is taken casually and begs for a second look. Now that we've been all the way around the Compass and you're getting a sense of who your inner Warrior is and what it takes a stand for, take a moment to re-glance at where the compass headings have taken us:

> **EAST:** *We entered the compass in the East, in the early morning, baptizing light, affirming purpose and potential. The path of possibility is clear to begin anew, again. Vision of what's possible and why it's important becomes clear.*
>
> **SOUTHEAST:** *We heard the gentle hooting of the Owl of Unconditional Love flowing outward with compassion and forgiveness, first to ourselves and then to all other beings. A commitment to a life of listening, curiosity and fascination is set.*
>
> **SOUTH:** *We are bathed, cleansed, and prepared for ushering in this new day from our wholehearted feminine nature. This is the home base of Warriorship. The inner healer arises, called to action with nurturing love.*

SOUTHWEST: *We affirmed our co-created path with the Universe and offer a profound prayer of gratitude. What we appreciate, appreciates. There is no doubt that we're on this journey together.*

WEST: *As the sun arcs overhead toward the sunset, we acknowledge the teacher in each moment, the opportunity at hand. Despite our fiercest inner critic, we remain open to outcomes, act intentionally and willingly let go of assumptions and clinging to any sense of permanence.*

NORTHWEST: *The Owl of Permission to Fail offers a hooting giggle at how tightly we hold ourselves and how unwilling we are to be anything less than perfect. As if messiness, shadows, and darkness aren't naturally a part of each day!*

NORTH: *The Warrior emerges. Choosing to show up fully, we step courageously into our masculine warriorship, rooted deeply and swaying easily with the windstorms of life. The sacred, prophetic arising of this warrior calls us forth with gentle urgency.*

NORTHEAST: *The Owl of Oneness hoots a reminder of our interconnectedness with all things. We let go of limitation as an excuse for not staying in our work.*

FATHER SKY: *We moved off the two-dimensional plane by looking up. From here, we see how we are full seen. We graciously embrace the responsibility to* *see others as we are seen. Nothing is deprived of this witnessing.*

MOTHER EARTH: *We looked below, to Mother Earth, the giver of all life. We take full responsibility for being good stewards of the land, the trees, the birds, the grasses, and all earthly resources.*

CENTER: *And we arrived here in the center knowing it intimately, and as if for the first time. We are grounded, centered, ready for what's ahead. We define what we are Warriors for and take a courageous stand for human resilience, determination, and creativity.*

We are all on this path and we are right where we need to be. Our life is indeed a sacred journey of adventure, growth, discovery, celebration, and transformation. Will you go forward, shaping your life story into a stunning tale? Will you arise with the Shambhala Warriors to protect our tribe, never mind the odds and ambiguity? Or will you go back to sleep, hoping the current comforts will carry you through? The pages of our story from here on are blank. There is nothing pre-written or predetermined for us. We get to write the story ahead.

At your center, you are a magnificent Warrior, equipped with everything you need to lead through the uncertainty, the chaos, and the dire consequences of doing nothing. I don't purport those things will change because you answer the call. But I do believe that, as I've heard it said, "God doesn't call the equipped, He equips the called."

I also don't make up a story that hope will necessarily win the day. But I do know that the Warrior's resolve to be in the fight is inextinguishable. The human spirit is indomitable. You are a Warrior, made for this time. You are ready to be of service and lead with courage. *"Stay in the center, and you will be ready to move in any direction."* Now be on with it, dear Warrior. Be on with bravely navigating the chaos, complexity, and uncertainty of the unknown as a warrior for the flourishing spirit of resilience and determination. We are with you.

EPILOGUE

On a flight to NYC in early 2020, sitting on the tarmac awaiting Air Travel Control approval to move, I suddenly realized this book needed to pivot. For the preceding 24 hours I was feeling more and more ill. Somehow my physical vulnerability opened a mental door to a voice I had been ignoring. It was a desperate longing for sanity amidst political chaos in the news. Listening to this voice I understood that something different was urgently needed. Little did I know at that moment how the world was about to experience something more demanding, scarier, and more disrupting than anything we'd ever known in our lifetime.

Originally when this book project began about the time I turned 50, it was created as a guide for thought-leaders to navigate their way in a vast and wondrous, but increasingly perplexing universe. It was a fun book to write, to share my experiences and hope they might help someone else. But abruptly I became hyper aware of how blatantly combustible recent events in the news were. This prompted the necessity to pivot the purpose of the book and the urgency to finish it. Having now experienced a year of pandemic induced uncertainty, the opportunity for doubling down on our centering practices is prescient.

I wrote this book with all the children in my life in mind—and their children, friends, and teachers. As life hurries along there is precious little space for sharing our depth with each other, much less leaving a legacy of guidance and wisdom. When they are ready, perhaps they will find this book waiting for them as a gift from my most raw, real, and sometimes disheartened self.

Increasingly, I find it difficult to put my best self forward when I haven't taken the time to get centered and grounded. And yet the desperate noise of climate collapse, systems failures, and disturbing political polarization is only getting louder, so I must find a way to keep ahead of the cacophony. The narrowed focus and purpose of this book emerged to help those who are looking to find sanity in a disrupting world to put their best self forward; to contribute in a meaningful way to the tiny pockets of life they influence; and to navigate the next step when hope seems a distant memory.

Take some time to listen to the silent spaces in your heart. Make room for words to arise from the stillness in those spaces. There, meet your best, most true self. Its Basic Goodness can no longer be squelched. Listen to your heart—it knows.

THE WARRIOR'S COMPASS STANDING MEDITATION

While I always start in the East, I often move through the model quickly and let one of the directions "call" me for deeper focus. This can take 3 minutes or 30 minutes. Sometimes I spend the entire time in the East. This is your practice, your day. Honor it as such. Stand facing each compass direction, literally, and shift your direction to each heading. Eventually you can add your own points of inspiration. Consider finding directional points on the walls around your room or finding trees as markers for each direction so you know where to focus.

Begin gently.

Bow into the space by leaning forward, hands at your waist, bending at your waist with reverence, giving thanks for the basic goodness present here. Raising your torso up, receive the many blessings of basic goodness in others.

Stand firmly on the ground, facing East.

EAST: Rising into the New Day: Feet shoulder-width apart, feeling them solidly on the ground. Roots from the bottom of my feet reach deep into the center of the earth. Hands low and relaxed. Chest open, shoulders back, face upward toward the early light. Soaking in the morning sunshine, I acknowledge Spirit's warmth within, feeling the first rays of bathing light on my skin. A gentle flame is lit under my feet from the soft morning rays and quickly builds into a cleansing fire throughout my body. The fire kills off all the brushy top growth of weeds from the day before but does not consume me. I accept Great Spirit's smile on this day. Burning even more deeply into the core of my being, the sun's white-hot flames baptize every atom of me with light, from my toes to the top of my head. On this new day, I begin again with a blank canvas on which anything is possible to be imagined. Basic Goodness is my core virtue. I was born at this moment in history to be here on this day. I re-member my life-purpose, letting it renew my calling into the day ahead.

Turning to the SOUTHEAST – The First Owl Flies in with Unconditional Love, Compassion and Gentleness: Standing with arms outstretched, palms facing the sky, and eyes gently closed; feeling a warm, orange-hued liquid filling up the body from the toes upward, pouring out the top of the head, then back down through the fingers, and the toes, overflowing into the whole room, the house, the neighborhood, the community, down every street and into every river, expanding to the whole country, across oceans, around the world and with increasing pace, into all space ... the stars, the universe and beyond. I am here to be a vessel of radiance – to give unselfishly and to love unconditionally. This starts with all that is good and flows through all of me: the beautiful, the shameful, the forgiven, the slightly awkward, the delightfully brilliant, and the ugly. All parts of me are included. Waves of unconditional love ripple outward, first to loved ones and family; then out to close friends; then colleagues, neighbors, and finally strangers around the world, touching every heart. I pause on each person, feeling loving kindness and compassion. May you all be healthy. May you all find gentleness in your suffering. May you all be resilient and comforted. May you all be happy.

Facing SOUTH – Opening the Feminine Heart: Feel the moisture all the way from the tropics wafting northward. Conspiring with the skies overhead to bring a warm rain that falls gently on my head, washes down my shoulders and arms, legs, and feet, dripping off my fingertips and out my toes, taking with it any residue of ash from the flames of the East. Drenched in these warm waters I am bathed by a source outside myself. The warmth creates a kind of Teflon mantle whereby anything that would attempt to attach itself to me (self-doubt, criticism, blame, low self-esteem, etc.) doesn't stick - it simply washes away. Cleansed, I hear a sweet, gentle voice, saying: May all my words be spoken from love, encouragement, and empathy, mending what needs mending and giving balm to a fearful and lonely world. I feel empathy for all of life, natural and human. I give myself to this day wholeheartedly – no reserve for fear, scarcity, or uncertainty. As a healer, I love and heal myself first. Baptized clean and free to give birth to a new day with clarity, inspiration and fresh energy, the waters flowing away from my feet grow into rivers and lakes and reservoirs of healing.

Moving toward the SOUTHWEST – Co-creating with the Universe: I am an integral part of something much bigger than "me." The entire Universe is working with me – creating my path just as I am creating it. I know that what I appreciate today will appreciate. No matter the difficulty, I carry beauty, gratitude, and confidence in my heart. Surrender into the flow of Life.

Turning WEST – Dreaming up the Sunset: Imagine the arc the sun will travel today, high overhead. Feel the rays of light blazing a trail of warmth from the bottom of the spine, up along each vertebra and up over the top of the head, lifting me up to be an inch taller. I stand on solid ground, claiming all that will be and how I want to feel at day's end. What might the day teach me? What do I have to teach others? Notice – be keenly aware of the assumptions that try to take root here. I am open to all outcomes and notice when I'm overly attached to them. I step into my brilliance. Fully embracing my potential, I know what is needed for today. Picking up a handful of earth, as if at the end of the day, I blow it all away with a simple breath. Everything I plan for, strategize about, and envision is held so lightly that I can still be open and allow everything to unfold naturally. Like a beautifully created Mandala that is created for this moment and then released, I feel present, light, without baggage and free.

Gazing Curiously to the NORTHWEST – The Second Owl Appears with the message of Full Permission to Fail: I give myself full permission to suck, to mess up and make mistakes today, and all the previous days I've walked this earth. I accept all parts of myself as necessary to be whole – light, dark, messy, brilliant and say a playful "ta daaa" when I fall into the inevitable muddy puddles and thank them. I embrace creativity, playfulness, and resilience today. I love you. I'm sorry. Please forgive me. Thank you.

Facing NORTH – The Warrior fully Emerges: The full extent of the brave, courageous and deeply compassionate masculine arises in me with a whoosh of frozen air. Today's accomplishments are infused with resilience, honor, and dignity. My back is strong and straight. I feel the wind pushing and pulling me about, but like Willow wedded to Oak, I am grounded by my deep roots and can sway with the wind effortlessly. I choose to show up fully present and give my best to every endeavor. I also choose to let my belly be soft, open, and vulnerable. Courage meets compassion in a graceful balance. I am life itself.

Turning to the NORTHEAST – The Third Owl Appears Proclaiming Oneness: Deeply grounded now, balanced in the paradox of polarities, dignified and open. I know that everything – large, small, known and unknown are interconnected. I am at one with everyone that comes into consciousness, every blade of grass, every bird's song, every grain of sand. I am you. You are me. There is no separation. We are one.

Looking UP to FATHER SKY – Fully Seen: Seeing all—being seen fully and transparently by the Great Spirit of the Heavens. The whole system is known, honored and purposeful. Help me to see as I am seen, love as I am loved and surrender into Your arms.

Looking DOWN to Honor MOTHER EARTH – Sustenance of Life: Holding hands outward in a welcoming gesture. Thank you, Mother Earth, for providing the very breath of life for every bug, tree, flower, seed, bird, animal, plant, and being. We are all blessed by your generosity, guidance, and abundance.

CENTER – The Secret Sits in the Middle: Left hand over right fist, two inches below the navel – this is my center. I notice where I stand is at the confluence—the co-incidence of heaven and earth. This is the place where humanity exists, connected above and below, supported and seen, never alone, never disconnected. And so, I bow to the Center where the perfect point of alignment exists. Gathering in all the energy from the Earth below… Gathering in all the energy from the Sky above… I bring it up through my body while breathing in – and pushing my breath out as I raise my hands to the sky. Then bringing all the energy from the Sky above while deeply breathing in, pulling it down through my body – and pushing my breath out loudly, giving it back to the Earth. Rubbing both fists on my lower back (kidney area) 3 times and with a loud "Haaa," releasing all energy into the Earth. I take in nothing extra. I am complete and have everything I need today. I rest in the Center of the compass, fully grounded, fully prepared, fully accepting of what is.

As I bow out, I offer gratitude for receiving the blessings of awakening. In seeing every part of myself and others, we are one. Thank you.